Sarah S. Baker

**Our Elder Brother**

thoughts for every Sunday in the year, from the life and words of Jesus of Nazareth

Sarah S. Baker

**Our Elder Brother**

*thoughts for every Sunday in the year, from the life and words of Jesus of Nazareth*

ISBN/EAN: 9783337255237

Printed in Europe, USA, Canada, Australia, Japan

Cover: Foto ©Lupo / pixelio.de

More available books at **www.hansebooks.com**

*"The First-born among many brethren"*

# OUR ELDER BROTHER

THOUGHTS FOR EVERY SUNDAY IN THE YEAR, FROM THE LIFE AND WORDS OF JESUS OF NAZARETH, BY SARAH S. BAKER

NEW YORK
A. D. F. RANDOLPH
AND COMPANY
(INCORPORATED)
182 FIFTH AVENUE

University Press:
JOHN WILSON AND SON, CAMBRIDGE.

*T*HE picture that we have tried to copy is the picture that we remember. Our results may be poor and disappointing, unfit to show to our nearest friend, but we have the original indelibly fixed in memory. Every curve of the outline, every delicate shade is ours.

So it is with the character of our Elder Brother. We try day by day to be like Him. Our imitation is a miserable copy indeed, but we have come to know and love our Perfect Example. It may even be that that wonderful transformation has been going on within us which will be perfected in the Better Home, when we shall "see Him as He is," and "know as we are known."

# CONTENTS.

## Before the World Was.

| CHAPTER | | PAGE |
|---|---|---|
| I. | Self-Sacrifice | 11 |
| II. | Creation | 14 |
| III. | Steadfastness | 18 |
| IV. | Humility and Obedience | 22 |

## A Child.

| I. | The Babe | 29 |
|---|---|---|
| II. | The Child Jesus | 33 |
| III. | Forms | 37 |
| IV. | A Name | 41 |
| V. | A Wide Circle | 47 |
| VI. | Boys | 52 |

## Ministering.

| I. | Temptation | 61 |
|---|---|---|
| II. | Babes in Christ | 65 |
| III. | Recreation | 71 |
| IV. | Seekers | 76 |
| V. | Tired | 81 |
| VI. | Relatives | 84 |
| VII. | Faults | 94 |
| VIII. | Mourners | 100 |

## CONTENTS.

| CHAPTER | | PAGE |
|---|---|---|
| IX. | SELF-DENIAL | 106 |
| X. | ECONOMY | 111 |
| XI. | OPPOSITION | 117 |
| XII. | DEFORMITY | 121 |
| XIII. | PARENTS | 127 |
| XIV. | SEEMING DEATH | 131 |
| XV. | THE NURSERY | 136 |
| XVI. | THE CAPITAL | 139 |
| XVII. | WORKMEN | 146 |
| XVIII. | CONSTANCY | 152 |
| XIX. | FORGIVENESS | 161 |
| XX. | TRUST | 166 |

### Crucified.

| | CRUCIFIED | 173 |
|---|---|---|

### Risen.

| I. | THE GRAVE | 177 |
|---|---|---|
| II. | IN REMEMBRANCE | 181 |
| III. | VISION | 185 |
| IV. | BY THE WAY | 188 |
| V. | THE OLD TESTAMENT | 193 |
| VI. | THE SHEEP | 198 |
| VII. | DAILY BREAD | 207 |

### Ascended.

| I. | LOST AND FOUND | 215 |
|---|---|---|
| II. | A MIRACLE | 219 |
| III. | UNION | 224 |
| IV. | DYING EYES | 228 |
| V. | A VOICE FROM HEAVEN | 231 |
| VI. | PERSECUTION | 234 |
| VII. | PENITENTS | 240 |
| VIII. | GENTILES | 244 |

CONTENTS.

| CHAPTER | | PAGE |
|---|---|---|
| IX. | Cheer | 249 |
| X. | Weakness | 253 |
| XI. | Priests | 257 |
| XII. | Churches and Church Members | 261 |

## Coming Again.

| I. | A Glad Welcome | 271 |
|---|---|---|
| II. | The Judge | 275 |

## In Glory.

| I. | Rest | 283 |
|---|---|---|
| II. | The Bride | 287 |
| III. | The Holy City | 290 |

Index according to Texts . . . . . . 295

# Before the World Was.

  I. Self-Sacrifice.
 II. Creation.
III. Steadfastness.
 IV. Humility and Obedience.

# OUR ELDER BROTHER.

## Before the World Was.

### I.

#### SELF-SACRIFICE.

*The glory which I had with the Father before the world was.* — JOHN xvii. 5.

WE can know nothing of the character of a human being, just born into the world. A babe lies before us a helpless riddle. His future development of body and soul, his gifts and his graces, are all to us impenetrable mysteries.

Not so with our Great Example. We hear of Him in the bosom of His Father before the world was. He had had an existence and a character already, in Heaven, before the opening of His career on earth as the Messiah. The New Testament, like the Old, goes back to the beginning.

We cannot picture the glory and the beauty and the holiness of the Heaven where the Only

Begotten Son was in sacred fellowship with the Father; that dazzling brightness is veiled from our poor human eyes. Of this one thing we are sure, our Lord was willing to leave that blessed Home and come down to the lost children of men. That "infinite stoop" gives us our first lesson in following Christ. With self-sacrifice His intercourse with man begins. His perfect joy was offered up that He might minister to and save mankind.

What have we to offer in return for His boundless love? Has not all that we have and are become suddenly precious to us?

Have you any special mental power or talent? It is to be used in the service of your Master. Have you worldly standing, or in any way preeminence among your fellow-men? From this day call it not your own. Be humble and modest and unworldly; be a brother or sister to the destitute poor, a loving messenger of offered mercy to the vilest of sinners. Have you rights to contend for? Is your own denied you at the hearthstone? Is some proper claim there overlooked? Lowly in heart, set aside your petty contentions; offer them all to him who offered all for you.

Riches! What are they? Passing dust of the earth, not fit to be trodden upon by the Lord of Glory! They cannot profit Him! Yet with them you can succor those whom the Lord has been pleased to call His brethren, even the hungry and the naked. Riches can even do the blessed work of sending willing messengers to tell the story of the Cross to "the nations that know not God." Your riches are no longer to be used merely to wrap yourself round with beauty and luxury, forgetful of the sufferings of your fellow-men. Not so can you follow the example of your Elder Brother; not so can you show your sense of His great offering for you.

What a glad thrill of heart when you can think of something more to give up for Him who gave up all for you! Your faults, your very sins, strange to say, have now a value. You can give them up, small and great, for Jesus' sake.

Every whole-hearted offering draws you nearer to Christ. Every gift is a fresh secret tribute of love, perhaps known only to Him.

Here begins a new stage in your Christian life. You are no longer your own, but your Lord's, — His with all you are or have, or can attain to; His for time and eternity!

## II.

## CREATION.

*All things were made by Him.* — JOHN i. 3.

WE have been allowed to have some knowledge of our Lord's occupations as well as His character before His Bethlehem birth. We hear in various places in Holy Writ of His delight in creation, in the exercise of the Divine power of making something out of nothing, of blending in delightful harmony beauty and order and utility and beneficence.

There is a natural longing to visit the Holy Land, where our Saviour walked in bodily form, and so to draw near to Him in loving adoration and human fellowship.

We need no far foreign journey to have present to us what has met the eyes of our Lord, what has been touched by His hand, fashioned by His wisdom, and adapted to the use of man. The light that gladdens us by day, the stars by night, the air we breathe, the welcome voices that reach our willing ears, the very friends that are dear to us, are manifestations of His love. Not merely the Holy Land has been trodden by His foot, but every atom of the round world is the work of our Best Friend! The whole organization of nature encompasses us about with mementos of His tender care "without whom nothing was made that was made."

If we would really know Christ, we must be reminded of him by all the loveliness and comfort and joy provided for us here below.

There have been loving hearts who in their devotion to their dead have left a room and even a home untouched, as it was last used by the dear departed. The whole earth is to us such a home, ever bearing the impress not of the dead but the living Lord! We are surrounded by works in whose creation He "had pleasure." When we study the physical laws of any department of natural science, we are coming into the thought of the Divine Being who formed them. Our earthly home is of His planning; and what a beautiful home it is for us, poor sinful children of men!

Every power we ourselves possess, whether of body or mind, is a direct gift from our Lord; and His is the gift to find satisfaction in the use of these powers. In trying to develop to the utmost what we have best in us, we are following out His faultless plan for our being; we are co-workers with our Lord. He gives us the innocent enjoyment it is to exercise the strong body and train it to grace and agility. He has made it a delight to the musician to group sweet sounds in pleasing accord, — to the poet to put great thoughts into words of beauty and metrical harmony, to the inventor to plan and execute, to the laborer to do skilfully his appointed task.

Whatsoever our gifts or our work may be, to use the one or do the other to our best ability is a kind of praise, a direct obedience to Him who has made the soul and body of each individual man. How this thought ennobles all labor, and sanctifies the highest as well as the lowest work!

And what has the beauty of the world made for man to say to us? He who made the bird to build his pretty nest for the bright fleeting summer days, He who has strewn the wild-flowers broadcast by the cottager's door, does not surely look disapprovingly upon our efforts to make our temporary dwellings here below tasteful and attractive, if we do not do it in a spirit of extravagance or ostentation. He would certainly have us mindful of the poor in the wayside hovel or in the crowded alleys of the city, in the miner's "cabin" or the factory village, and do something to make their homes neat, comfortable, and refining. He must look with pleasure on the kindness that prompts to adorning the sick-room of the invalid, the convalescent ward of the hospital or insane asylum, or even the nursery for the little ones, so beloved by the Good Shepherd.

We cannot create. Our tools of mind or body, as well as our materials, are the gift of God. We may, however, with the powers of which we are possessed, group the materials to which we have access in some new manner that may minister to beauty or utility in this our lower home. We may help to scatter, where we pass on our earthly way, what may gladden the eye or cheer the heart or ennoble the soul of our fellows. For the possibility of such lowly following of our Lord, without whom nothing was created, we shall be called to account!

## III.

### STEADFASTNESS.

*The Lamb slain from the foundation of the world.*
Rev. xiii. 8.

SELF-OFFERED, our blessed Lord was "the Lamb slain from the foundation of the world." Men may be capable of great deeds in a season of high enthusiasm, or through the long maturing devotedness that finds its sudden climax in a moment of daring unto death. We cannot conceive the infinite love and compassion and fixedness of purpose which could enable our Lord to look forward through long ages to His great humiliation and supreme self-sacrifice.

It is from our Elder Brother's unswerving resolve to be offered the Great Shepherd for the sheep, that we must learn the patient continuance in well-doing, the ceaseless pursuance of noble aims, the unflinching cutting off all that may lead us from God and holiness.

It is written that the Master, "for the joy set before him, endured the cross, despising the shame." Even higher joy than He had known with the Father (and we may gather even higher honor) was pledged to our Lord in that He was willing to humble himself and take upon Him the form of man, and be on the cross the one great offering for the sins of the whole world. We, too, are not without the promise of an exceeding great reward. Not that our poor services are to have wages. Wages are for sin, — even the death that is wrapped up in evil doing! The *gift* of God is eternal life; and this eternal life of joy is promised to all who will accept free forgiveness in Christ, and strive to follow His example of love and purity.

We have also, in our little measure, something to look forward to, from which human nature shrinks. We have the hour of death, the one thing of which we are certain in our otherwise veiled future. Here we have the deep sympathy of our Lord, who Himself passed through the valley of the shadow, and has "tasted death for every man." He knew through rolling centuries upon centuries just what was in store for Him. He knows as well just when and where we shall lie down and die; and He has in reserve for us the sustaining strength that is to bear us through that trying hour. The nearer we live to Him now, the better it will be for us then.

Days or months or years may lie before us ere we leave this our earthly path. He to whom "a thousand years is as a single day," will be our strong consolation through all the vicissitudes of the way!

"Thine own friend and thy father's friend forsake not," says the Scripture proverb; and how we cling to those who have known and loved us from childhood, and have loved our parents before us! Such friends do not turn coldly from us in the hour of trouble or humiliation.

But what shall we say of a Friend who has "loved us from the foundation of the world"? He has known us in advance as none other can know us, with all our sins and our backslidings; and yet He has loved us with an everlasting love! He has chosen us for His own! He who has so loved us will never forsake us! In Him we may have "strong confidence!" The wild waves of earthly commotion may be tossing around us — we are safe with Him who "holds the waters in the hollow of His hand." He will not let us sink in the billows of temptation, if we but cry to him, "Lord, save us!" He loves us with an old, old love. Before Abraham lived his mortal life, we were dear to our Lord, of His children in the faith, for whom He was willing to be the Crucified Saviour!"

There are times when a sense of desolation and loneliness creeps over us. We seem walking in darkness, and fumbling in vain for the warm hand of friendship to give us its cheering grasp.

Do we forget the "Friend who sticketh closer than a brother"? Have we honestly tried to have the bond close between us and our Lord? Have we sought His friendship and companionship as assiduously as we might that of an earthly associate whose affection was precious to us? Have we conformed our tastes and habits and wishes to His, as we would to those of a beloved human friend?

May we so love this unchanging Great Friend, that we may live in the glad remembrance of His presence, and grow in His likeness, and have His illimitable help in every hour of need!

# IV.

## HUMILITY AND OBEDIENCE.

*My Father.* — JOHN xiv. 7.

AS in botanical studies, so in biography, it is not only the flower and the fruit we examine, — we must know also the parent root.

It is not to David or Ruth or Abraham that we turn to find the spring and fount of the perfect character of the man Christ Jesus. He had truly in His nature gathered up all the nobility of the long line of His earthly ancestors, down to that maiden, "blessed among women," who was honored to be the mother of the promised Messiah. But this Saviour of the world was not merely a man; He was Emmanuel, "God with us." He whose "compassions are new every morning," who of old had "not despised the afflictions of the afflicted," the pure and perfect Almighty God, sent to the fallen world His Only Begotten Son, the "express image" of the God of Love.

How incomprehensible to us is the humility of the Son of God! How the pride of the human heart is humbled in His presence!

With what eager interest we read of our own forefathers, and proudly flush at their achievements, as if we, unborn, had had a share in their merit! Our own family pride we can always tolerate, or excuse, or even indulge and foster. An exhibition in our neighbor of this same family pride, how unacceptable, how repulsive it is to us! We seem to desire to occupy ourselves a pinnacle upon which few can stand,—a point from which we can look down on less favored mortals. This is not the innocent, honorable, natural satisfaction in the merits of those who are allied to us by blood. This is a seeking of our own honor. Men must hear of our claims, that we may shine before them with a reflected light.

There is a radical cure for this spirit in the faithful following of our Elder Brother. The Son of God, "full of grace and truth," comes not to us to claim the exclusive right to the honors of sonship and a home in the "Father's house." He wills that we shall be with Him where He is. To them that overcome will He grant "to sit with Him on His throne."

Wandering, sinful, unworthy as we are, He would lead us to the Father's house, freely forgiven for His sake. Believing ourselves orphans, waifs, or erring children who have forfeited their inheritance, and hunger far astray, He comes to us with the assuring words, "Your Father which is in heaven." He gladly tells us that the love of the Father never fails, and that He is ready to receive us, and even to come out to meet us and welcome with great joy His repentant children.

What a lesson this is for us, proud despisers of the lowly, haughty teachers of the fallen, niggard dispensers of help to the needy!

If we would learn at the feet of Jesus, and truly follow His example, we must put aside at once our pride, whatever form it may assume. We must draw near to our Elder Brother simply as sinners to share in His redemption, and to walk lowly in His footsteps. Our Lord is not only full of yearning love towards His sinful brethren, we are told of His obedience to His Father.

The will may be broken or bent to the wishes of another by punishment or fear; but only love subdues it and moulds it to spontaneous obedience. Our submission to our Heavenly Father must not be that of the down-trodden slave to a cruel master, or a servile subject to his earthly monarch. It should rather be the glad yielding of the will to that of the Best Beloved, stronger, wiser, and holier than ourselves. Such obedience makes the fulfilment of the law an exceeding joy.

In many of the great natural forces and forms of creation there is much that we cannot fully understand, yet they can be adapted to the use of man. So the great mystery of the free obedience of our perfect Lord can come with its wholesome lesson to us poor revolted subjects of our Heavenly King. Dwelling on His loving submission, we may learn to pray sincerely, as we are taught, "Thy will be done," before "Give us this day our daily bread."

It may well be said, "The will dies hard." It springs early to life in the babe, and is still strong in the tottering old man.

It is our earthly lesson, knowing the will of God to do it instantly, constantly, lovingly, whatever it may cost us. The words "So I come to do thy will, O God," should be the reverent expression of our inmost wish and aim. We may humbly add, "For this cause came I into the world." "I myself am here in mortal form to be fashioned by cheerful obedience into the likeness of my Lord."

Human beings have but rarely an opportunity for any one great conquest of the will. It is rather by the daily, cheerful submission, in a free and loving spirit, to small trials that beset our commonplace life, that the soul is trained to a childlike obedience. Scarcely an hour passes that we may not accept some little uncongenial duty, some passing pain, or trifling injury or loss, in the yielding, gentle spirit that trains us to be the true servants of God. These little sacrifices can nurture no secret pride, as if we had done some great thing. They are, therefore, less dangerous for us who are so easily puffed up, "as if we were somewhat."

Perhaps we may not dare, with our poor wavering purpose and many inconsistencies, to say the sacred words, "Lo, I come to do thy will, O God!" The prayer, "Teach me to do thy will," offered from a sincere heart, will surely be abundantly answered.

# A Child.

   I. The Babe.
  II. The Child Jesus.
 III. Forms.
  IV. A Name.
   V. A Wide Circle.
  VI. Boys.

## A Child.

### I.

### THE BABE.

*The babe lying in a manger.* — LUKE ii. 16.

NEVER to our knowledge did the Lord Jesus more fully show the perfection of His sonship than in His willingness to shroud His divinity in the form of one of the most helpless of new-born creatures, — an unconscious babe.

He who in his manhood was powerful in prayer, and could by a word have summoned legions of angels to His aid, consented to begin His mission on earth unable to utter a single petition. He was to depend upon human beings for daily care. An inexperienced girl was to be His mother. He was to be defenceless in the midst of the world He had created. In the Father of all was His supreme trust. He would be watched over in His weakness, and be enabled to grow in grace and stature until the time of His "showing unto Israel."

"My Father and your Father," so the Lord spoke of our Almighty King. Why should we fear to cast ourselves wholly, body and soul, earthly cares and heavenly hopes, upon this unchanging Friend? We are no longer helpless infants; we have the power of prayer and the promise of help through prayer. "The Almighty arms are under us." Let us lie peacefully and quietly there, sure to be borne safely through all that is before us. And our dear children, for whom we have so many anxieties, let us trust them to God, as Jesus trusted Himself in infant form, sure of the superintending care of the Father. Let us give our children wholly to God, to be His and His alone, and believe that He will grant us wisdom and strength to train them for His service.

Even we, poor mortals, have a tenderness for those who are passing through the same experiences by which we have been tried. A well-known millionnaire gathered around him the little newsboys of one of the world's largest cities. When the joy was the highest he said to those struggling children of poverty, "I was once a little newsboy, like you." He could make no long speech; his throat swelled, and hot tears filled his eyes. His heart was warm towards those little waifs, and they knew it. Their hearts beat strong with answering love for him who had once been like them, and knew so well how to feel for them.

We can dimly think how every babe that is born into this world is to our Lord a memento of the Bethlehem Babe, who lay helpless in the manger. No wonder that He loved, when on earth, to take little children in His arms and bless them!

And what has a babe become to us? Even as the cross, a sign, an image, a reminder of the loving humiliation of our Lord. Christians have felt as if they were expressing their devotion to Christ Jesus by wearing a cross on their breasts, or humbly kissing the sign of His crucifixion. We have a living image of our Lord, which we may clasp to our bosoms and caress and care for in memory of Him, — even the babe that comes helpless to the world in which Christ was born a human child.

The son that we love in his infancy may prove to us a cross of pain, through his misdoing, for he is of the seed of Adam; but we need not despair of his final salvation. He whose grace seeks the prodigal in the far country and brings him home to the Father's house, He who pardoned the repentant Magdalen and the thief on the cross, can bring our wandering children at last to the blessed fold. Let us be instant in prayer, faithful in teaching, pure in example, untiring in patience and love, and trust to God as to how and where and when our sons and daughters shall be brought home to the Good Shepherd.

## II.

## THE CHILD JESUS.

*Thy holy child Jesus.* — ACTS iv. 30.

LITTLE children begin their lives as preachers and teachers. We have them in their infant years as hints of what our Creator meant us to be. They have truly upon them the taint of Adam; but we get through them still an inkling of his state in the happy garden. But what an atmosphere is this into which they come! Even the best of Christian homes is no perfect place. The most saintly of parents give no faultless example. The seeds of evil, that seem to have scarcely life in the tender infant's soul, find congenial surroundings in which to grow with a rapid and rank luxuriance. They are fostered too often by the jarring tones of the very mother's voice and the fretful, angry concert of brothers and sisters in contention. What a responsibility it is to be in daily intercourse with a little child!

The tender little ones in baby years are our living sermons. In them we find the utter unworldliness that bows down to no station, and responds to the smiles of the lowest as to the condescensions of the crowned head. The atmosphere of love is all that the little ones crave, and when they find it, they give freely responsive love in return. They are ready to kiss the hand that chastened them. They bear no malice, they suspect no evil; they give to the uttermost, and gladly. Things have no factitious value to them, — grains of gold and sand of the seashore are equally precious to them. They have no past to regret, they fear no future. They live like the plants in the dew and sunshine, and grow unconsciously in grace and beauty, to gladden the beholder. God be praised for the little children!

This beautiful evidence of what our nature might have been we see even in our little ones, born of sin-stained parents, but what must the Holy Child Jesus have been!

The heart thrills at the thought that human beings were privileged to see and love such a little one. What must it have been to behold linked with such perfection the humility that touches us in ordinary childhood! Let us bow low before Him, our Infant Master, and learn the great lesson. We do so want to be something, or seem like something, or to do some great thing, or to seem to do some great thing. There are men who would rather be called great sinners than to sink into utter insignificance. To be born among humble folk and cradled in a manger would not be at all to their taste. To be saints in high life suits them better. This is a claim they are never willing to yield. Let these would-be saints compare themselves with the Great Pattern.

He who, "being in the form of God, thought it not robbery to be equal with God, . . . being found in fashion as a man," could be the little child in the carpenter's home, submitting to being managed and controlled by the humble pair for the time set over him!

There are few persons in the organization of our civilized society who can be said to be wholly independent. The body politic has its parts, which must fit into one another. Each works under some higher power, or must be judged and controlled in a measure by his peers. How men chafe at this subjection and supervision! What heartaches result from mortified pride, and unsubdued wills ignored or thwarted! Let us be like our Pattern, the Child Jesus, subject to them that are placed over us in the providence of God. Let us serve our Heavenly Father faithfully, though it may be in an obscure corner He has placed us, and look to Him alone for the approval of our work. It is the humility that accepts its appointed place in life, and labors conscientiously there, that wins the precious commendation, "Well done, thou good and faithful servant! Enter thou into the joy of thy Lord!"

## III.

## FORMS.

*Thus it becometh us to fulfil all righteousness.*
MATT. iii. 13.

IT is sometimes fancied that the spiritual life is most pure when it can dispense with all forms and all ordinances. There are Christians who claim that they can worship best, not in the sanctuary with their fellow-believers, but in the quiet chamber, or on the hillside, or in the woods, alone with God and Nature. They crave no outward sign, they say, of the grace given unto them by the Holy Spirit and dwelling in their hearts.

This is not the lesson taught us by the example of our Elder Brother. The beginning of His earthly life, and the opening of His career as the Messiah, were marked by the acceptance of the ordinances prescribed for Jewish and Christian believers. He who knew no sin was circumcised in His infancy, and baptized in His manhood. The Lord Jesus and His disciples were frequenters both of the temple and the synagogue. The Master assembled around Him His chosen followers to eat of the Paschal feast, and Himself instituted the simple supper to be taken in memory of Him.

Surely it becometh *us* "to fulfil all righteousness." Through whatever means God has promised to bless us, those means should be to us precious. Souls that are hungering and thirsting after righteousness will not willingly neglect any God-sent manna by the way, any springs provided for their refreshment on their heavenward journey. They rather wait upon the Lord according to His appointment, and leave to Him to send a rich blessing to His obedient children.

Through the whole ordering of nature and grace, means are granted for desired ends, a container for a thing contained, a medium for the transmission of the most subtle influences. This we cannot explain, but so it is. We can send our message to our friend across the wide ocean; but it must travel down in the deep water along its allotted path. The loved voice that speaks to our glad ears from a distant city is not borne on the wings of the fitful breeze. Its way is along the mysterious line that the ingenuity of man has stretched beside the common road, or through fields and woods, by homesteads and villages and towns, to link heart to heart, and head to head. for the courtesies and friendly interchanges and the great business affairs of life.

It is when the container is put before or instead of the thing contained, the means before the sacred end, the form before the reality, that the outward ministrations of religion become dangerous. The nature of man is so prone to rest in externals that he must ever be on the watch against this danger. A so-called prayer may be a worthless form, when it is thoughtlessly read from the printed book, or glibly spoken by false and fluent lips. It may, too, whether written by saints of old or spoken from the momentary promptings of a devout heart, be such a real cry of the soul to God as insures a flood of blessing.

The Bible may be read as a tiresome duty, or in a critical, carping mood, or in a state of listless indifference. It may, too, be sought as a comforter, an adviser, a guide, and a pure channel for an influence that lifts the soul heavenward, and fills it with a spiritual joy that makes this life a glad pathway to the better home.

The Sabbath may be a time of cold and rigid observance of religious duties,— a penance to the young, and a bondage to the old. It may be, as well, a day of growing in the spirit of love to God and man, a taking a new strong step heavenward, a refreshment to soul and body, and a foretaste of the rest and gladness in the Heavenly City.

The sacraments may be dangerous, outward,

soul-destroying forms, or they may be to the earthly pilgrim to the Land of Beulah wells of water and the bread of life that nourish him with angels' food.

Let all means prescribed for growth in the religious life be welcomed in the spirit in which they are given, employed in the way appointed, and in the remembered presence of the Great Giver, and they will be found sure channels of that grace which sanctifies the willing soul!

## IV.

## A NAME.

*Thou shalt call His name Jesus.* — MATT. i. 21.

IT is delightful to think that in heaven there is not an inseparable mass of rejoicing angels and glorified saints, but a collection of individuals with their own peculiar characteristics and distinctive names. There, Abraham is still Abraham, and Moses Moses. The holy men of old have simply passed from life on earth to life in heaven. Even the angels, when sent on special messages to man, have been allowed to tell their sacred names, and we may so think of them personally and individually.

What name our blessed Lord bore in the glory He had before the world was we are not permitted to know. An angelic messenger from heaven declared the name that was appointed Him as the Saviour of mankind, even Jesus, the name above all others for the believer's ears.

When we name our children we doubt and hesitate. The living great man, after whom we would call our son, may so sin that he will be cast out from society, and his name be a shame to the helpless child. Even the friend whom we have trusted, and whose name we would give our boy, may prove our enemy, or be to us as an indifferent stranger, and the sound of his name in the family circle be a source of poignant pain.

We give our children names, as it were, in the dark. We know not what manner of children they may be. We cannot hope to have their names descriptive or especially appropriate.

The name of Jesus could well be given before His birth, for He came to save His people from their sins. He was to be the Universal Healer of the universal plague.

Not by one name alone do we know our dear ones on earth. Love contrives all sweet names by which we breathe our affection for our nearest and best beloved. The Bible is starred all over with inspired names by which we may know our Divine Friend, as He comes to help us in all our human needs. We may think of our Lord as the Shepherd ready to seek His wandering, helpless sheep. He is our Captain in our strife with evil, our High-Priest with His one perfect offering for all mankind. Yes, we may not dwell on the more than three hundred names by which our Lord, in His manifold tender relations to us, is described in the Sacred Scriptures. To seek out and meditate upon these names is one way to know our Master more intimately, and draw near to Him with more loving confidence. So shall we begin to understand how He meets every want of our souls. So shall we grow in love to the name Jesus, which comprehends all, as it brings the dear Lord before us personally, as the one we love best, our comfort, our confidence, our joy!

May God give us grace to see and know Him as He is! Since the followers of our Lord were "first called Christians at Antioch," they have borne the name of Christ, which should pledge them to "depart from all iniquity." Many of them have nobly redeemed this pledge, by pure and faithful lives, by a martyr's death, by unflinching steadfastness in the midst of strong temptation, by warmth and zeal when surrounded by worldliness and indifference in the Church itself, by cheerful submission to sore affliction, by noble devotedness to the sick and suffering, — yes, by truly following the Great Example in all boldness, in all holiness, in all simplicity, and in all humility! Of such men and women the world is indeed "not worthy," yet even the world gives them its tribute of praise and makes their names symbolical of the virtues they have most strikingly represented. Who does not know what is meant when the word of praise is, He is a Paul, a John, a Polycarp, a Howard? or, She is a Mary, a Dorcas, a Monica? All along the centuries, noble men and women have stood out as patterns of some form of Christian excellence, and their names have been adopted into common language and have helped to keep up the idea of what man ought to be, by showing what man has been.

We cannot hope that our names will pass into this honored vocabulary, yet all of us who bear the Christian name embody some form of character to the little circle to which we belong.

Perhaps most of us would be painfully surprised to know what we really represent to the cool, critical, clear-sighted outside observer, who is not blinded to our peculiarities by party feeling or personal affection. The man who considers himself an eloquent preacher of the Gospel may be reckoned an unfaithful shepherd, who will not himself lead his flock in the path he points out, and whom it would be madness to follow in the way he treads. He who counts himself the champion of others' rights and a pleader of the cause of the down-trodden may be stamped as the ambitious self-seeker! The woman who calls herself shy and sensitive may be the touchy and self-conscious, "minding her own things" instead of "the things of others." She who would be known as the friend of the poor is rather characterized as the busybody, who puts herself forward, caring more for her own prominence than for poverty or the poor. She who thinks herself friendly, kindly, and hospitable may be the seeker of admiration and the praise of men, willing to help all outside the family, but cold, disobliging, and indifferent towards those bound to her by the ties of blood.

There is one name which belongs most truly and certainly to us all,—the name of sinners. "The blot is on us!" We cannot escape it! And yet this name is in one way our safety. Christ Jesus came to save us from our sins. He died for sinners. We may come humbly and penitently to the mercy-seat, and plead the name above all others, and be forgiven and "accepted in the Beloved!"

There may be a "new name" laid up for us in heaven. We may be already written by that name in the Book of Life. That name may express that we are "saved as by fire," or that we have "resisted unto blood, striving against sin," or that we have been "conquerors through Him that loved us." That great secret of the far future no one now can know. That name may tell the timid follower, who has almost feared to call himself of the family of Christ, that he has been a dear child of his Heavenly Father in the midst of his trembling upward walk. The puzzled doubter, head-wrong and heart-right, who in a pure life and an earnest seeking of the truth has been "faint but pursuing," may find that he has been as the blind, whom Jesus was leading, though he knew it not.

When those new names are read, the lowest in his own estimation may find himself the highest, — "the first may be last and the last first." Then, be our crowns shining with many stars or dim with the shadows of our earthly past, we shall cast them down before the Lord, who has bought us with His blood and has given us, unworthy children of men, an abundant entrance into His Heavenly Kingdom.

## V.

### A WIDE CIRCLE.

*We have seen His star in the East, and are come to worship Him.* — MATT. ii. 2.

OUR Saviour was, in His teaching and in His life, both democratic and cosmopolitan. Not that it was His object to overturn existing forms of government. Loyalty, not lawlessness, is the spirit of the Christian religion. Our Elder Brother was democratic in the sense that the distinctions of life — high and low, rich and poor, socially respectable or simply repentant — were as nothing in His sight. At His very entrance into this world, this tendency was emphasized. He lay in the manger of a wayside inn, a carpenter His foster-father, His mother a humble young woman, made a wife through the loving pity and firm faith of her betrothed. To simple shepherds, pursuing their modest calling at night, bands of angels announced His coming.

A Jew by blood and birth, limiting the scene of His earthly ministry to His native land and condemned to death in the sacred city of His people, He was yet, from the beginning of His career below, to be not only the king of the Jews, but the Redeemer of all mankind. He reverenced the law and institutions of Israel's race, and so loved the doomed capital that he cried out with tears, "O Jerusalem, Jerusalem, how often would I have gathered thy children together as a hen gathereth her chickens under her wings, and ye would not! Behold your house is left unto you desolate!" Yet in Him all the families of the earth should be blessed. He was not the prophet or Messiah of one people only, but the ends of the earth should praise Him! That lone star that guided those seekers of truth from the far East to come with their offerings to the stable of Bethlehem was the first flash of the light that was to lighten the Gentiles, and the promise of the distant day when all nations should bow the knee to Jesus, and lift up to Him united prayer and praise. How constantly,—by direct teaching, by miracle, and by example,— our Lord rebuked that selfish kind of patriotism which would arrogate to itself all honor, and all claim on the Divine blessing, to the contempt of outside strangers and foreigners, and their exclusion from the partaking of the richest blessings of Heaven!

The spirit that limits the circle of true Christians to this cluster of believers here, conducting their public worship according to this established rule, clothing their priests precisely so at the altar, celebrating this feast in this authorized manner, or giving that doctrine the supreme pre-eminence, is quite foreign to the spirit of the Great Founder of our religion. The glad revelation of the Gospel of love and self-sacrifice comes to us with a freedom that fits it for all times and all nations. Many are the vessels and many the forms that can convey its life-giving essence. Away with the narrowness that divides brother from brother by the church walls, which to Him who sitteth in the heavens are but as are to us the irregularities on a polished surface, invisible to the naked eye. Let us love and give and praise, walking in the purity of God's law, and accepting the great redemption through Christ, for all who will believe on His name and follow His example!

True religion begins in the family, making dearer every tie of blood, and through love obliterating self and joining master and mistress, children and servants, in one glad household, walking heavenward together, each in its place, but without pride of place, or murmuring rebellion, or servile obsequiousness. Where love reigns there are order and obedience and mutual help and sympathy. Such households are the little temples in which the Great High-Priest is ever present.

After the family comes friendship. He who loved Martha and Mary and Lazarus, and companied specially with Peter and James and John, understands this need of the human heart, and provides for its innocent gratification. He gives that Christian love and fellowship which can make the room where two or three are gathered together in love and prayer, as well as where many are joined in the great congregations, as the entrance gate of heaven!

But true Christian love is not shut up to the domestic hearth, or limited to the circle of friendship. It is like the fountain that leaps to the sunlight, and scatters refreshing drops not only on the rich greenness that encircles it, but on the thirsty grass far and wide, and refreshes the air for the weary passenger who but sees in the distance its sparkling beauty.

It is a poor, narrow Christianity that does not find its way to the poor, the ignorant, and the wicked, and to the "nations that sit in darkness and know not God!" True Christianity makes true patriotism a thing not of selfishness or ambition, but, in an enlarged and wider sphere, the carrying out of all that is loveliest in family life. It has, too, its friendship for outsiders, a large and loving recognition of all that is noble in other lands, and a willingness to grant them their due meed of honor, and to insure them

# A CHILD.

their due share in the blessings of civilization and religion. Such friendship recognizes that the swarthy African and the subtle dweller in Eastern magnificence, the sturdy men of the frozen North, the listless loungers of the isles of the sea, have hearts like our own, the same loves and dangers and death. Do they not need the chief joy of life, the comfort of the sick-bed and the house of mourning, the light when the world grows dark in the shadow of death? Let the light to lighten the Gentiles shine in every land! In zeal and self-denial, in loving generosity, let the Christian nations join in sowing the good seed beside all waters!

## VI.

## BOYS.

*And He went down with them and came to Nazareth, and was subject unto them.* — LUKE ii. 51.

"WHAT shall I do with my boys?" is the anxious question of many a mother's heart. If there were unlimited truth in the saying that "The boy is father of the man," well might the mothers despair. Happily, there is much in the wild, mischievous, thoughtless nature of boys that passes away with early youth. There is much, however, in the cast and drift of character that always will remain the same, even though the child should early have the best of blessings, the beginning of a true Christian life.

There was one mother who knew no anxiety as to the development of her son. She could be sure that He would grow in wisdom as in stature, and "in favor with God and man." She had no strange budding plant, entrusted to her care,

## A CHILD. 53

that might yield a beautiful fragrant blossom, or possibly a poison flower. She had no mere human child in her keeping. She was "blessed among women." Her boy was the Son of the Highest, Emmanuel, who should save His people from their sins, and whose kingdom should have no end! What joy must have filled her heart when she looked upon her perfect child, and dimly foreshadowed the great future before Him!

Once she sought Him sorrowing, not that she could fear that He had gone astray from the path of holiness. She was to find Him already about His Heavenly Father's business, but ready to go down with her to Nazareth to be the obedient child in the carpenter's home.

What a comfort it is to know that Jesus is "the same yesterday, to-day, and forever." He has had a boyhood of His own. He has lived among boys and knows their nature and their temptations. He was tempted not only "like as we are," but like as they are, yet without sin. When all human friends have lost patience with an erring boy, we can think how tenderly our Saviour, who understands so well to what boys are exposed, looks upon the offender.

"Christian mother, go with your prayers for your boys to the Lord Jesus! He knows better than you do the peculiar faults and temptations of your son. He can make you wise to rule and guide him. He can give him the pervading influence of the Holy Spirit to quicken his conscience. He can be to him "as a wall around him by day and by night," to preserve him from the dangers that threaten him from without and from the sins that are surging within. Mothers, lean on the Lord Jesus, and go patiently and hopefully forward. Go forward patiently and hopefully, but still actively. Mothers may and must fold their hands in prayer, yet not in indolence or despair. Here, as everywhere, faith and works are inseparably linked together. There is no promise that your children are simply to be borne heavenward on angels' wings, while you look admiringly on, or busy yourself as pleases you best, either inside or outside of your home.

The plants that minister to our bodily necessities need care and culture. The crops that fill the garner and feed the hungry do not grow on the neglected hillside, but in the fields cultivated by the toil of man. Human beings are given to human parents to be cared for and trained and educated. Their very helplessness keeps them near to and dependent upon father and mother, at an age when the young of the beasts of the forests are free rovers by wood and flood.

The first years of a child are all your own.

Begin at once to mould him for a pure life on earth, and a bright future in the Heavenly Home. Be methodical, be gentle, be firm with him, from the very first. Let the boy be early taught good habits, and to be subject to your will, as to food and sleep and cleanliness, before his own will can assume the mastery over his fleshly habitation. Give him an atmosphere of love to grow in. Keep him happy by your cheerfulness, let your smiles prompt his own. As soon as he can fold his hands for thanksgiving, associate that thanksgiving with his daily food. Let him early remember to trust himself, loved and forgiven, to the care of his Heavenly Father for the night, and wake to thank that Father for peaceful sleep and a new day of blessings.

But we cannot follow with the mother that child's pathway through life. For her, while he is under her care, there will always be self-sacrifice in the present and the future. She is no longer her own, since she has become a mother. A tender child-hand, visible or invisible, is always drawing her, often when she would be wholly free. It is written, "She that liveth in pleasure is dead while she liveth." This is even true of the maiden, in her glad days of girlhood. Mere pleasure is not the end of any human life, at any stage, though much innocent joy may be, and should be if possible, the portion of all God's creatures. A mother, however, has turned her back upon self-indulgence in any form, when once her little one has been laid in her arms.

How we are moved at the thought of that mother swept away by the overpowering flood that destroyed a whole town, — borne off by the wild waters, her children clinging about her. Clinging they still were, dead like the mother, when stranger hands took them tenderly from the wasting deluge, and strong men's tears fell at the sight.

Such scenes we perhaps see unmoved around us. There are mothers dead in pleasure, with children "dead in trespasses and sins," fast clinging to them. Poor little children, who have mothers who cannot forego the follies and pleasures of this life, to give time and thought and love and wise, tender care to their young families. How can such mothers expect a self-denial and patience from servants, which their own natural affection is not sufficient to prompt? It is generally the neglected children who break the mother's heart, or bring her to shame by their misdoings.

The self-sacrifice of the mother does not end in the nursery. There it merely begins. If you would have your boys in any way like the Lord Jesus, be to them at least a Christian friend, who loves their society, and moulds them to pure tastes, holy thoughts, and a blameless life. Be what you should be, and be much with your boys, ye dear mothers, who would lead those boys to happiness and heaven.

# Ministering.

I. Temptation.
II. Babes in Christ.
III. Recreation.
IV. Seekers.
V. Tired.
VI. Relatives.
VII. Faults.
VIII. Mourners.
IX. Self-Denial.
X. Economy.
XI. Opposition.
XII. Deformity.
XIII. Parents.
XIV. Seeming Death.
XV. The Nursery.
XVI. The Capital.
XVII. Workmen.
XVIII. Constancy.
XIX. Forgiveness.
XX. Trust.

# Ministering.

## I.

### TEMPTATION.

*He Himself having suffered, being tempted.*— HEB. xi. 18.

A PERSON who has been surrounded from childhood with the refinements and restraints of a high form of civilization in a Christian land cannot but be shocked and outraged by finding himself in the presence of sin in an unabashed and flagrant form. The same sin may have its essential root in his own heart, in selfishness or hate or irreverence or in the inability to control bodily indulgence, yet it may still be abhorrent to him in its ultimate and full development.

Even more painful is the awakening to the fact that the once despised sin of the open evil-doer is now to him a temptation, is gaining ground with him, is perhaps taking the mastery, and binding him a hopeless victim.

We, poor human beings, can have a horror of sin, but we have no real conception of its true danger and malignity. We cannot measure the humiliation that it must have been for the nature of the Lord from heaven to be blended with the being and organization of a child of Adam. It is true that He was tempted yet without sin, yet He must have "suffered being tempted." We can understand how this mysterious experience draws Him near to His struggling, tempted brethren, and how exactly He knows how to adapt His sustaining grace to their needs in their lifelong contest with evil without and within. He is and ever must be touched with a feeling of our infirmities, and ready to stretch out to us the helping hand.

What is usually called "the temptation of our Lord" was a special experience at a definite time. It is recorded how He triumphed in that conflict, and it is added, "The devil left Him for a season,"—for a season only, it seems. Of his future assaults we know nothing. The life of our Lord has its own secret history, and so it is with all those who strive to follow His perfect example.

Only our Lord Himself knows how and where His chosen saints have their most bitter struggles. Of this one thing only we can be sure regarding our fellow-Christians: if they be Christians indeed, and growing in the likeness of their Master, they "suffer being tempted."

While temptation is suffering, there is always hope for a human soul,—there is still left a trace of the image of the God to whom sin is abhorrent. When conscience has been silenced by the power of evil habits; then indeed is the soul threatened with a sickness unto death. The fools who "make a mock at sin," and laugh at their own wickedness or that of their companions, are far gone in the dark downward path.

Do you shrink pained from finding in yourself the slightest worldly motive or ambition, or bowing of the heart to riches and high station? Do you see its meanness, its opposition to the Bible precept to be no respecter of persons? Then you may still hope to escape the love of the world, which cannot exist with the love of the Father in heaven.

Is your most trifling departure from truth a cause in you of shame and real repentance? Then your lips may yet be made free from guile, and from the thing which God "hates," even "the loving and making a lie!" Is a foul word or story uttered in your presence a repulsive source of pain to your inner consciousness? Then you may yet be of the pure in heart who shall see God.

When you have ceased to suffer from temptation, and from even the slightest consent to sin, the battle for you is well-nigh lost. Rouse yourself to renew the conflict before it is too late! Keep near to Christ! Remember His presence, and your conscience will grow tender by such association and such remembrance.

Watch over your little children that they fall into no such habits that any form of temptation shall cease to be to them a source of pain. Bad habits rob temptation of its suffering. Good habits help to keep the conscience alive and active. Oblige your child to do right, if you cannot perusade him to do so of his own free will. Form his tastes and his habits, and pray that God may give him the inner life, that will make those habits an expression of what he most desires to be. Walk yourself blameless as far as you can, and so you will do your part to keep yourself and him sensitive to the evil of sin.

## II.

## BABES IN CHRIST.

*And He called unto Him whom He would, and they came unto Him.* — MATT. ii. 13.

BABES in Christ! It is a scriptural expression, not merely the language of man. Nay! Man would rather represent that the true Christian, really born again, must have attained at once to the perfect measure and stature of the follower of Christ. Nor is this an unnatural mistake. There is so unspeakable a difference between life and death that even the new convert himself, in his joy at the great change that has passed over him, is tempted to believe that he who has been chief of sinners has suddenly become chief of saints.

Here the wise caution is necessary: "Let not him that girdeth on his harness boast himself as he that putteth it off."

The babe is a wonderful thing, a new creature. It is a being born to be developed to noble manhood, an heir, if he will, of a life of endless joy. Well may there be gladness in a home to which such a little one has been sent by the Heavenly Father! Yet the child's life is at its beginning. It can only be rejoiced over as a babe.

So it is with the beginners in the heavenly walk. True Christian hearts throb with glad thanksgiving when another soul is born into the kingdom. There is even joy in heaven over one sinner that repenteth. Such beginners must remember, however, in the midst of their exuberant transports, that humility is the crowning virtue of the Christian life.

How different is the babe with its helpless body, its unawakened heart and dormant mind, from the noble man with his muscularly developed, stately form, guided and governed by the will within, — the heart with its deeply rooted affections, the mature mind with its culture and its mighty power to know and understand. Yet they are one and the same being at different stages of existence, the individuality never lost, the full, mature beauty wrapped up in the poor infant, less able to supply its own wants than is the flower to open to the dew and the sunshine.

The saint in the new Jerusalem may be as unlike the same saint on earth as is the babe to the strong man, and yet he will be himself, through all the stages through which he may pass, an individual being, created and developed through the almighty power of the God of Love.

In the babe in Christ there may be infolded a blessing to mankind. Let him but remember that he is at the beginning of his course, and humbly and modestly, with prayer and patience, tread the Christian walk, ever looking to Him who has given him this new life to sustain and unfold it to full fruition.

The Jews who came out from the multitudes who thronged to hear the wonderful words, they who listened to His call and joined themselves to Christ, He was pleased to reckon at once among His followers. Yet how He instructed and warned and reproved them, and even the chosen twelve who were with Him by day and by night, and constantly heard the blessed words that proceeded out of His mouth! How faithless, how human, how far from sharing their Master's spirit were they, one and all! Yet He did not cast them out. Let us learn from the love and patience of our Lord to welcome warmly the beginners in the Chistian life, and not to expect a sudden perfection in the jaded sinners who have just cast off the yoke of the world, the flesh, and the devil. Let us be glad that they have set their faces heavenward. Let us be careful that our wandering footsteps do not lead them from the right path. Let us strive to surround them by loving sympathy, and help them by a faithful, consistent example.

You who walk in your uprightness, and would condemn your fellows as unworthy members of the Church of God, beware lest you are scorning one of the "little ones," the babes in Christ, struggling towards a stronger life! Make them feel that they are a part of the body of Christ, dear to all its members, and dear to the great Head Himself. The babe in the family is the object of the tenderest care.

In taking our nature upon Him, our Lord became part and parcel of us all. With what divine compassion He regards those of His children who have just awakened to a new life. He will well know how to foster that life and bring it to maturity. Let Him deal with His own. Help if you can in the spirit of a devoted elder sister or brother, not of the impatient stranger or of the harsh heathen who would cast out the weak and sickly babes to a certain death.

And you, beginners in the heavenly walk, do not be content to be always babes. You must grow, or you will be dwarfed, deformed, or droop perhaps to a hopeless death. Growth is by food and exercise and rest and tender care. This care the Shepherd has promised to His lambs. The food you know how to obtain. You know how to have your needs supplied. Use the means of grace. Lean on the ever-present Saviour. Do the duty of the hour. Walk conscientiously, courageously, consistently, and for you is the path of the just into the perfect light.

Be patient, mothers, with your little children who lisp of "love to Jesus," and a desire to "be good," and yet are so full of childish faults and shortcomings. Do not despair of them. Do not taunt them with insincerity, because their expressed wish to be lambs of the flock is so soon followed by conduct that is far from lamblike. Let them see that you trust them, and believe in their sincerity, while you must point out to them their faults, and visit them with wholesome discipline or deserved punishment. Let them feel that you would in this way carry out their earnest wishes, so confidingly expressed.

And you, young Christian, who are ready to lose courage, and doubt if you are in the way of life, because your sins are so many, and your character is so ill-regulated, do not let these signs of babyhood make you doubt whether you are living. Your very heplessness and danger may lead you to trust more entirely and humbly to the Great Friend, to guard and guide you. It may be growth and development you need, not life. If you want to be a child of God, want it with all your heart as your chief desire, cherish that beginning of a new life. The Lord Jesus stretches out His hand to such as you. Take it! take it firmly and walk by His side in prayer and faithful practice, and you will grow out of babyhood into the sure and happy life of the true children of God.

# III.

## RECREATION.

*And both Jesus was called and his disciples to the wedding.*
JOHN ii. 2.

OUR Lord is welcomed to the funeral and the house of mourning, but how few bid Him to their feasts or would have Him at their merry-makings! We seem to class Him with those friends whose slumbering tenderness towards us is drawn out by our afflictions, but who cannot rejoice in our happiness.

Sorrow, in whatever form it may come, is in the eyes of the world a kind of humiliation. From the height of their better fortune, the honored, the happy, the successful may look down in a kind of complacent pity on the mourning, the disappointed, the sick, and the suffering. Not so with our Lord.

If you fancy you love your brother, your friend, your neighbor, question yourself whether you are filled with glad sympathy when he has some sudden joy or honor or success. If you ask yourself the question in the presence of God, the All-knowing, perchance you will be obliged to murmur the "God be merciful to me a sinner!" of the conscience-smitten publican.

Our Lord Jesus when on earth was not a friend only for dark days. He could stand by the grave of Lazarus and weep with the sorrowing sisters, but could as well be present at the wedding at Cana of Galilee, an honored and welcome guest.

In our deep realization of the solemn mission of our Lord to this sinful world, we are too apt to forget that He came as an image and expression and embodiment of the God of Love. The morose reformer is not likely to be bidden to feasts where his presence is only a gloomy shadow, and his countenance as a threatening cloud. We may be sure that even in His holy purity this was not the impression made by Him whose "compassions are new every morning." There was sunshine about Him, or the mothers would not have thronged around Him with their little ones, the despised sufferers would not have looked trustfully to Him for help, the outcast sinner would not have turned to Him for pardon.

We seem to fancy that God made our eyes for tears, and that from some other power came their glad twinkle of merriment, or their expression of innocent joy, in the midst of social converse. Who wreathed the mouth with smiles that answer to smiles? Who made the dimples to come and go in the baby's face? Who lit the glad, loving light in its eyes, as it begins to be aware of the tender care of its mother?

Why will we not remember that joy is as much the gift of God as sorrow, and to be as freely accepted in His presence? We will hold fast to the heathen idea of the Most High, and think we must "cut ourselves before Him," and rob ourselves of light and hope, to be His acceptable worshippers.

In the beginning of His earthly ministry our Lord gave an open protest against this conception of the Friend of Sinners, while at the same time He stamped His approval on the glad honoring of the institution that sets men in families. Later, He was not slow to express plainly His sense of the permanence of the marriage tie. Our Saviour sanctified the mutual duties and the sacred joys of home.

As parents should dare to be innocently happy in the presence of God, so should their children be encouraged to let their natural joyousness have vent at the side of father and mother. When all the merriment and gladness of the little ones is shut up to the nursery, or only let loose on the playground, or in the secret haunts of the children, where schemes of mischief are plotted and planned, a dangerous gulf is yawning in the home, a gulf that may ultimately cut off the little ones from the affectionate sympathy, the tender counsel, the wise guidance of those whom God has set over them for good.

There is a worm in the rose when it does not open to the glad sunshine. There is danger in the joy that shrinks from the companionship of the wise and good. That is a false happiness that cannot be welcomed as a gift of God.

Amusements have come to be dreaded as a power for evil, because they are too often an expression of a desire to escape from the lawful restraints of soul and body, that are absolutely essential for true and lasting happiness.

There are so-called amusements that are indulgence in questionable pleasures, or are the well-known road to open sin. Here the rule should be, "Touch not! Taste not! Handle not!"

There are many amusements, in themselves innocent, that are most dangerous when they tempt pleasure-seekers to make them the business of life. There are some people who are like children who would ride the hobby-horse all day long, to the utter neglect of all proper lessons and all prescribed occupations.

Some amusements may not be objectionable in themselves, but made dangerous indulgences because the sharers in them are not sufficiently self-controlled, not sufficiently pure, to avoid making a destroying poison of what should be an innocent recreation.

There are still other amusements that ought to be high and ennobling, but public taste makes them ministers to folly and prompters to sin.

When we harshly condemn this or that amusement, perhaps we should more justly blame our own hearts, or the spirit of the social circle of which we are a part, — which our own tastes and principles do their share in forming. Let us all dare to be both inwardly and outwardly what we should be, happy children of a Heavenly Father, and the question of lawful amusements will be simplified for us and our families. We shall so help to make it possible for others to enjoy necessary recreation, without being sullied in heart, or unfitted for the appointed duties of life. We may cut off this indulgence, and this place of amusement, and that diversion, and this style of reading, all perhaps, in the present state of things, reprehensible, but this cutting off will not prepare us for innocent amusement, unless the heart is so purified and the will so directed that we can be naturally happy with the remembrance that we are in the presence of our Heavenly Friend.

Let us accept gratefully all blameless enjoyment, and accept it ever as given of God.

## IV.

## SEEKERS.

*Nicodemus, which at the first came to Jesus by night.*
JOHN xix. 39.

THERE is perhaps no way in which we could better judge of the real character of a distinguished man than by noticing the manner in which he received the various persons coming to him for aid or counsel. How often, in mere human beings, there would be something of pride of place, or consciousness of superiority, or affected condescension, or selfish indifference, or the deep-seated worldliness that has an ear and a smile for the prosperous and great, but a haughty disdain or a hasty rebuff for the downtrodden or the needy.

It is in our dealings with men at large that we show what we are. It is sometimes a sad surprise to one who has found a stranger congenial and attractive in a *tête-à-tête*, to see that same person in other society, echoing or accommodating himself to the tone of thought of the vicious or of the open scoffer.

The unchangeableness of our Lord — the same always in love and purity and dignity — cannot but strike us as we follow Him in his intercourse with all states and conditions of men. When the ruler Nicodemus came as a seeker of truth to Jesus, but secretly and by night, he met no cold rebuke. He was given freely to drink of the living waters, blessed words were spoken to him, on which we Gentiles, at this remote day, delight to dwell, as the bulwarks of our faith and our strong consolation.

Our Lord gave loving and gracious answers to Nicodemus, but He did not fail to add the great lesson for all puzzled seekers, that the dawn, if it be indeed dawn, must end in the perfect day. It is the man ashamed of his earnest search after truth and holiness who is unwilling to let his fellow-men know that he considers such a search the most important aim of a human life. It is only he who is walking in the law of God, as far as he knows it, and living in purity and sincerity while seeking immortal truth, who can hope to find light, and rejoice in its life-giving beams.

Far down in the ground the seed may be quickening, or shooting patiently upward through the dark soil, but this is but the beginning of life. It must eventually up to the sunshine, the dew, and the free, pure air, if it is to blossom and bear fruit for the pleasure or profit of man.

There are souls that in their conceit and self-sufficiency are determined to find out a new path heavenward for themselves. They will be indebted to no man, not even the Man Christ Jesus! The old trodden path of repentance and humility is not to their taste. They will not even knock at the gate of heaven. They would step boldly in, claiming a right there, on account of their human perfection. This is, alas! a well-known class of so-called seekers of truth.

There are persons who close their eyes to the light because their inmost heart cannot bear its pure rays. The lives of such persons generally show in the end why they have been so averse from the exactions of the pure law of God. They have set their faces towards the outer darkness of those who turn their backs on God and holiness. On this form of unbelief we must look with deep pain and sorrowful pity. From the baleful influence of such unbelievers we would gladly shield those puzzled doubters who would willingly find themselves in the ways of faith and peace.

The tender dealing of our Lord with Nicodemus comes with its comforting whispers, when we think of those seekers of truth among the wise heathen philosophers of old. There may even now be lovers of truth, justice, and purity, far from the light of the Everlasting Gospel, who may be beloved by Him who opened the eyes of the groping beggars at the gate of Jericho.

Sometimes an experienced Christian finds himself in a mist as dark and chilling as that which suddenly surrounds and bewilders the Alpine traveller. He seems entering into a dreary night of doubt and despair. Such a state of mind may spring from many causes. It may arise from some mere physical derangement that for a time clouds the understanding and dulls the heart. The yielding to some powerful temptation may have changed the attitude of the soul towards God, and left the voyager, before going steadily onward towards his goal, like a ship drifting anchor in a wild storm on a strange sea. Such doubts may spring from the slow undermining of Christian character, through a too eager pursuit of lawful pleasures, or the chilling influence of a worldly atmosphere become congenial, or from the cruel seeds of unbelief, wilfully and skilfully planted by some daring infidel.

From whatever causes such a state of mind may arise, it is night to the soul. In such a night there is but one help, — to go simply to Jesus, like a little child, telling Him of the trial, and seeking His all-powerful aid. This is no real unbelief, to be met by the examining of evidences and the study of Church history. This doubt is pain, as of estrangement from a dear friend. It is not disbelief in the existence of that friend, or of his claims to confidence and affection. Such a suffering Christian, in the midst of his confusion of mind, would endure much persecution, and perhaps even offer his life, rather than range himself among the enemies of the cause of Christ. If such doubters truly go to Jesus, in their night of trouble, there is a bright dawn in store for them. Repentant, forgiven, received again to the near companionship of the Master, they will go onward and upward, fearing nothing so much as the possibility of losing in any way the light of His countenance whose presence is fulness of joy.

## V.

## TIRED.

*Jesus being wearied with His journey.* — JOHN iv. 6.

IT is astonishing how little we hear of the personal discomforts to which our Lord was exposed. He too could be weary in this toiling world. He too could long for rest, and seek the quiet mountain-top or the desert place to be alone with His Father.

There is a weariness which overtakes us all at times, in the midst of active life, and prompts an overpowering desire to get somewhere, to have some refuge, if but for a day, when not even an hour of solitary peace can we dare to claim. Such is often the weariness of the mother, with many young children about her. She is exhausted by nights of wakefulness beside an uneasy babe, or by watching some little sufferer, or by the very restlessness of the ever-moving, ever-changing group about her, of which she must be the centre and the irresistible attraction.

There is no escape for you, faithful mother, but there is a loving smile of approval for you that could cheer and strengthen you, if you could see it with your mortal eyes. Jesus, who so loved little children, loves them still, and values your every effort and sacrifice. He does not think, because you go over the same duties day by day, that they cost you nothing. He knows your every weary moment, and all your thronging cares. Let His love and sympathy help you to go bravely on. The time is coming when the little ones about you will be strong to love and strong to labor. Even here, on earth, a great reward may be in store for you!

And you, busy father, sacrificing personal ambition and even the exercise of your highest mental gifts, in some plodding calling, where you win daily bread for your dear ones, what wonder that you are sometimes wearied with the journey! Sit down, then, by the well whence the living waters are to be drawn. Look to your Heavenly Friend! You are doing the work He has planned for you, and you have His approval. Your character is strengthened and ennobled by your every sacrifice. You have a present reward in the tender love and unbounded confidence of the helpless group entrusted to your care, and a better reward, when your earthly labors are over.

There are many weary pilgrims, but all may have the same consolation. Life is indeed a journey, but, unlike most other journeys, it has no fixed, known, and clearly appointed close. It may last for long years, it may end to-night!

What does the traveller in a strange country care for passing inconveniences when he fancies he is near his last station. He keeps watchful and ready for the change. His ears are open for the words that may be the summons for him to leave his fellow-passengers and the comforts and discomforts of the way. Perhaps there is some friend gone before who is waiting to meet him, and eye to eye will flash love, and hand will grasp hand, telling of unchanging affection. What, indeed, to such a traveller are the small annoyances by the way?

"Gird up the loins of your mind," pilgrims to a better Home! Think of Him who has prepared a place for you in the heavenly mansions. Live much in the thought of the Friend who is to meet you "beyond the river." So will you be insensibly fashioned into His likeness and into fitness for the Home which awaits you when life's long journey is over!

## VI.

## RELATIVES.

*And when Jesus was come into Peter's house, He saw his wife's mother laid and sick of a fever.* — MATT. viii. 14.

OUR relatives by birth we have generally known from childhood. The familiar intercourse of years has created in us that sort of attachment that comes from mutual interests and the exchange of necessary courtesies and kindness, even where there is no real congeniality and no very near blood relationship.

We accept as we must the members of the home circle, love them heartily and naturally in most cases, and in all make the best of them. Family quarrels are universally condemned, and there is fixed upon them a certain measure of disgrace. The Scriptures go farther and enforce family affection as a duty, as well as a privilege and a source of the purest and most lasting earthly joy.

As by common consent, mankind rebels more stubbornly against the uncongenial relatives with whom human beings become connected by marriage. There is a noble as well as an unworthy ground for this difficulty. The loving, loyal heart is repulsed by the idea that persons, often utter strangers till met at the wedding feast, should at once be accepted on a par with the dear ones of house and hearth, linked with a whole past life, and near through strong and grateful affection as well as by the natural bond.

There is often, too, a similarity in the modes of thought, the perception of duty, and the aims both for the inner and the outer life, in a whole family connection. The bride or bridegroom may be suddenly plunged into an atmosphere quite new and uncongenial, to have long cherished preferences and prejudices perpetually shocked. The feelings may be wounded and the taste offended because these strangers, who are at once brought so near, are themselves playing upon an unknown instrument, meeting on a familiar footing fellow-creatures of whose habits of thought and peculiarities of character they are quite ignorant, or which they are wholly unable to appreciate.

For all this there is a slow but certain cure in the open-hearted willingness of the bride and bridegroom to accept their new relatives as they find them, not as they fancy they ought to be. As a plain matter of fact, these relations are grown-up men and women not to be made over or remodelled to suit a new young member of the family. They are to be taken and loved and cherished and made happy, in the spirit of frank friendliness, in Christian submission, and in whole-hearted unselfishness, though it may not be easy to take at once quite near to the heart these strangers, who must be called by the sacred names of father or mother or sister or brother.

These real difficulties in accommodating one's self to new relatives, which are so often met and conquered by the warmth of a loving, conscientious nature, are quite different from the cherished opposition, the sharp-eyed spirit of criticism, the mean, small seeking for opportunities of difference, that may be found on one side or the other in the new relation. The bride and bridegroom are sometimes so selfishly wrapped up in each other that they consider the outer world only worthy to exist as far as it can conform to their wishes, or minister to their already abounding happiness, or at least not in any way intrude upon or diminish their unspeakable bliss. Such selfishness at the beginning of married life may make permanent strangers or even enemies of those who would gladly have taken the place and office of near and affectionate relatives. Even a mother or father or sister or brother, who cannot cease to love the selfishly absorbed offender, may feel repulsed and thrown off, and grow stiff and ceremonious with one who has been dear to them as the apple of the eye, blood of their blood, and heart of their heart.

Into whatever household or family circle the Saviour has truly entered, the Friend of all and transforming all into His likeness, such animosities, such opposition of interests, such bickerings, can find no place.

We know nothing of the moral condition of things under Peter's roof at the time of our Saviour's appearance there, which is honored by the mention of three evangelists. That Peter's wife's mother was a member of his family shows that there was a strong bond of love or duty or congeniality between them. That the Master was at once taken to her bedside on His arrival indicates an eagerness that she should profit by the healing power that He was ever so lovingly ready to exert. Her sickness is called a fever, a "great fever" by one of the narrators of the incident. The physicians of our own day speak of a fever as if it were an enemy to be met and defeated by a nice system of tactics. Our physicians must often work in the dark. They know much of family matters, but they are not father confessors, to whom each member of the household may fully open the heart. There is much that causes and sustains disease, into which the wisest physician may not be able to penetrate.

Who knows what anxieties may have preyed upon the mind of Peter's wife's mother? How wild, erratic, and unpractical she may have thought him, to be forsaking his boats and his nets to follow the new Master, who after all had only promised to make him "a fisher of men." She was perhaps familiar with the household difficulties consequent upon his course. The future of the family perhaps lowered gloomily before her. She had a vision of the wife and children sitting deserted in a home of poverty, while the husband was madly following the new Teacher to strange cities.

Who can say that Peter, with his hasty tongue that could even rebuke the Lord Himself, may not sometimes have wounded her to the quick, by a sharp criticism or a bitter retort, and made her feel that a home in his house was by no means a bed of roses. Perhaps she had no confidence in "this Nazarene," and had not cared to meet Him. Now she lay on her bed sick with a fever. She was not to be asked what physician should be brought to her side.

Our Lord came like no ordinary physician to seek out symptoms and sound body and soul. He knew all the patient's pains and weaknesses.

He knew her trials and her sins. He came not on an official visit, for so much pay, so much experience, or so much renown. He came full of ability to heal, and of love to understand and forgive. What a visit that was from the Great Physician! He took the patient by the hand and lifted her up. He lifted her up, doubtless, both in body and in soul!

"There went out virtue from Him." She felt that loving confidence in His willingness to help which His presence seemed so marvellously to inspire. Here was just such a friend as she needed, one who came with a kindly touch of the hand, and a deep sympathy for her in all her troubles!

So our Lord is willing, even now, to come to every sick-room and every troubled heart. If, like the wise surgeon, He cannot always spare the sharp knife, or dull the agonizing pain, He can give courage to bear the worst torture, and to triumph in the sorest mental struggles.

We need not say He will come to every lowly patient. There is no sick-room so dark that He is not already there, willing to give His wonderful light. There is no sufferer so lowly that the Friend of the poor is not ever beside his bed!

If man would but turn in his distress to the Great Physician, not despising the means He has graciously appointed, but looking to Him for a blessing on all means, and for support in all suffering, what a different world this would be!

We read of the patient, Peter's wife's mother, that Jesus "rebuked her fever and it left her, and immediately she rose and *ministered* unto them." That was a sign of a recovery of body and soul that does not always appear after illness. How often the contrary effect is produced by being the centre of interest and attention on the sick-bed and during convalescence. Who has not seen the faithful servant nursed through pain and danger to become an imperious mistress in her exactions, or the little child tenderly cared for by anxious love until it is a domestic tyrant? We may judge of our real gratitude for our recovery by the use we make of the life newly given back to us, or the lost strength so mercifully restored.

In our extremity what weary watching fell to some one's lot for our sake! By what patient, thoughtful service we were nursed back to life! In what spirit have we risen from the sick-bed? Have we a more tender feeling for all sufferers? Are we querulously ready to insinuate that this or that invalid has brought on himself by thoughtless imprudence the pain of which he complains? Have we become so used to being waited upon that we have ceased to remember

## MINISTERING.                                   91

that hired feet can be tired as well as our own? Have our hearts and our purses fully and freely opened to relieve the poor who languish in sickrooms that are the family resort, the family workshop, the family dormitory, and the family nursery?

What a joy it must have been to Peter's wife's mother, after her sudden recovery, to be allowed to minister to the Master, as a revered and beloved guest! Now she understood Peter's enthusiasm for Jesus of Nazareth! She needed no longer to fear because her son-in-law had left all to follow the new Teacher. In His care Peter and Peter's house were safe!

We have not the Lord to minister to on our recovery, but if we have caught His spirit we shall find it a delight to minister to the needs or contribute to the joy of high or low, rich or poor, friend or acquaintance, as the opportunity may providentially be afforded us. We shall be a new source of help and happiness in the home in which our lot is cast.

In the times that are gone by, family affection rarely allowed the sick to be entrusted entirely, or any more than was absolutely necessary, to the care of a hired nurse. Such a nurse was then too commonly an ignorant if a willing help, and sometimes an incompetent mercenary or an irresponsible drudge. Then it was customary for friends to supplement the exertions of the overtaxed family of the patient, by sitting with the sufferer by day, or watching beside his bedside at night.

That time has passed, and as to nursing, the trained and capable Christian women who now devote themselves to this self-denying occupation can in most cases give far better care to the sick than the nearest and most devoted relatives. This is now everywhere acknowledged. Yet this very fact is bringing evils in its train. The sick-nurse is so kind and competent and acceptable that the family of the patient, relieved in a measure from anxiety, and feeling themselves superfluous in the sick-room, go on with their ordinary occupations, cheerful, and often indifferent and forgetful as regards the sufferer, who finds the nurse truly very agreeable and capable, but feels himself living in a dreary world, apart from all he holds most dear, and apparently as easily dispensed with as a worn-out glove. Such is human selfishness, that this may even happen in families accounted lovely by outsiders, families in which business and pleasure and self-indulgence are the ruling elements, rather than true affection linked with deep Christian life. In such households it seems to be taken for granted that the sick-nurse has supernatural powers. She is supposed to need no rest, day or night, no recreation, no cheering social chat, no friendliness, no fresh air. It is as if she were bound to perpetual self-abnegation, and almost to a slow self-murder!

These things ought not so to be! The good sick-nurse does not come into the house to foster pleasure-seeking, worldliness, and selfishness.

There is a ministry for all of us in our homes and in the homes of others, in sickness and in health, in joy and in sorrow. Not sickness alone, not recovery, can teach us this lesson. The Lord Jesus must take us by the hand and lift us up, and give us of His loving spirit, and then we shall arise and minister unto our fellows, after His example and in His name.

# VII.

## FAULTS.

*Why are ye so fearful?* — MARK iv. 40.

NEVER does our Lord seem nearer to us than when He lies in the little vessel on the Sea of Galilee, fast asleep, like one of ourselves. From the deep rest of weary human nature, He is not even awakened by the roar of the tempest about Him. We see in Him here our Brother, who could suffer fatigue of mind and body, and sink overpowered into the forgetfulness and unconsciousness of kindly sleep. So it seems to us now, but to the disciples that sleep was almost like wilful desertion. Jesus was their Master, to whom they looked for help and guidance. In His power they were beginning to have unlimited trust. Now He had laid aside his sceptre, and seemed lost to them in the hour of trouble, even unmindful of them and their needs. They dared to wake Him, and address to Him the words of wounded confidence and almost indignant reproach.

The majesty and power of our Lord crowned

Him on awaking. The winds and the waves were hushed into subjection. They who had presumed to rouse Him from His quiet sleep felt Him now an august stranger, and whispered timidly together, "What manner of man is this, that even the wind and the sea obey Him?"

What did the disciples expect the Master to do, when they roused Him to come to their aid, if they were so astonished at the execution of His sovereign power?

What a picture we have of the Church of God, and even of individual believers, in those few men in the storm-tossed ship! "They cried unto the Lord in their distress," but were filled with stupefied surprise and timid awe when He heard and answered their prayer.

There are few ways in which Christians show more their lack of real faith than when they stand astonished at a direct answer to their prayers. In our troubles we besiege Heaven for help and add in our hearts if not with our lips, "Master, carest thou not if we perish?" Yet we are hushed into convicted silence when the sudden answer to our prayers overtakes us, perhaps as we rise from our knees.

Real answers to prayers are not only a rebuke to our latent unbelief, but a strengthening as well to our atom of faith. We have seen what manner of being our Lord is, and more truly than ever before rely on Him with childlike trust. In such a response to our cry, we have perhaps a secret with Him alone, which we should shrink, it may be, from naming to mother or sister or brother, yet it sends us singing on our way.

It is not to all Christians that the question "Why are ye so fearful?" can with the same pertinence be addressed. Individual character sets its stamp on the spiritual life, its joys and its difficulties and its temptations. Peter is born Peter, if not in name, and John is born John. We come into the world with fixed characteristics, and probably each with his peculiar bias, his weak places, where the enemy may most readily make his assault.

This fact is most important for the educator to remember, be he parent or teacher. A child's natural gifts and tendencies must be patiently and prayerfully studied, by one who would guide and direct and develop him aright. There may be points of character about which even the mother of a boy may be long in doubt, while others will be clear to her from his earliest infancy.

There is no characteristic that shows itself more early than timidity. Some children, from the dawn of opening consciousness, are fearless and confiding and friendly. Others shrink from strangers with a quivering lip, and lay the head on the mother's shoulder, they know not why. Some baby faces will cloud and fill with tears at a harsh word, while others will answer frown with frown, and hasty reproof with irritated opposition. How few children have pains early taken with them to soften and modify their dangerous peculiarities!

There is a time when a human being comes into a new possession of himself, as something given back to him, as Moses was to his mother, to be trained not like Moses for an earthly princess, but as a voluntary subject of the King of Kings. Bought with a price, we are no longer our own, but pledged to live in the midst of this evil world in accordance with the laws of Him who has bought us. The beginner in the Christian life sees in himself an instrument to be used in his Master's service. What is the temper of that instrument? What is its appointed work? He hardly knows its strength or its deficiencies. On a careful examination he is discouraged, humbled, cast down. He seems made up of incongruous elements, diseased, out of joint, imperfect at every point. In the midst of this natural and suitable humiliation he should take courage. Every human character is an uncompleted work. It is not to be judged of until the last ingredient, the essential ingredient, is added to the composition. The cure for the apparent disease must be applied. The hand of the Master must set right the disordered machinery. The Power that is the secret of all growth must develop what is imperfect or existing only in the hopeful germ.

Our very faults may be for us the source of our virtues, if subjected to the healing touch of the Great Physician. Have you an anxious, timid, shrinking nature that you think unfits you for a true soldier of the Cross? You are weak that you may be strong. Natural courage, headlong, thoughtless bravery, even to rashness, can stand abashed before the courage of a Heaven-sustained Christian woman. Such women, in the strength that cometh from above, can face danger and certain death with a calm and cheerful offering of themselves for a high purpose that ranks them among the noblest and bravest of earth. The fearful who flee to the Lord in their felt helplessness, have a source of courage that is inexhaustible. Let them take heart, and answer the self-reproachful question, "Why are ye so fearful?" with the comforting words, "That because we are fearful, knowing our own weakness, we may so flee to the Lord and trust in Him only, that no anxieties, no coming pains, no threatening dangers can disturb our peace!"

So we might make the round of human frailties

and shortcomings and special temptations. "Man's necessity is God's opportunity," here as elsewhere. Our faults, our very sins, may be made the prompters and sources of our virtues. The place where the fort was known to be weakest has been made its strongest point. The struggle, through God's grace, with our known enemy, may make us excel where we have most frequently failed. The tried and tempted may not only be the forgiven and reformed, but the rescuer of the falling and the fallen, and the glad finder of the lost and despairing.

## VIII.

## MOURNERS.

*He had compassion on her.* — LUKE vii. 13.

THE human heart has a deep craving for sympathy and compassion. Why else does the invalid recount his pains and the mourner tell her tale of sorrow though it costs her a fresh outbreak of bitter tears? There is a desire that others may know what we have suffered, that may even become a morbid craving, as in the case of a well-known afflicted child, early developed in the spiritual life, but not purified on earth from human weakness. As he looked at his little wasted limbs his plaintive voice pleaded, "Let my friends see my body when I am dead, and then they will know how I have suffered."

We may smile sorrowfully at that poor petition, but we all have within us the germs of the same spirit. Yet we feel it as a weakness, for there is in uncomplaining sorrow a majestic power that appeals to every heart.

Our Lord was ever ready to hear and respond to the prayers of the sick or their friends, yet His divine compassion seems to have been specially touched by the silent grief of the widowed mourner beside the bier of her only son. His tender sympathy for that desolate woman was not only to cheer her heart, but to be a stay and comfort for bleeding human hearts down the long centuries, until all the redeemed should come to that home in which God shall wipe away the tears from off all faces.

"The Lord's compassions fail not. They are new every morning." He stands by the bier with the sorrowing. He still says to the eyes blinded with tears, "Weep not!" "I am the resurrection and the life!" Here we have the full satisfaction for our natural craving for sympathy. No human being is so desolate or so isolated that the Great Comforter is not beside him. No sorrow is so secret that He does not know it in all its bitterness. No affliction is so crushing that He cannot lift up the head and the heart of the bowed mourner.

The afflicted may cry out in his anguish even to the friends that would console him, "Miserable comforters are ye all." The words of dear sympathizing brethren may sound in the ear like dim, far-off bells, that summon him whither he cannot come. The voices of even the living beloved ones seem outside the sorrowing heart, and powerless to hush its pain. The Lord Jesus with His compassion comes into the heart, takes up His abode there, and whispers a peace at which the world must wonder. He can give in the darkest hour a foretaste of the blessed time when "sorrow and sighing shall flee away."

The son of the widow of Nain, waked from the dead, "sat up," and the Lord "delivered him to his mother."

That same Lord will not indeed now wake our dead and give them bodily to our loving arms. Yet in His own way He takes our treasures from us, and yet delivers them to us again. As they are in their heavenly home they are given back to our loving hearts, — all blemishes blotted out, all shortcomings forgotten, they are forever enshrined in our memory. We love them here below, we cherish them with the love that can cover a multitude of sins. We see no faults, we remember now no failings in the dear one in heaven. We see him as God meant him to be, as he wished to be, and as he now is. He is delivered to us again, as one of the "just made perfect," and so we treasure his image. The light of heaven has fallen on the face that we loved, the heart that was so near to ours has been fully washed and made pure in the blood of the Lamb. It is as if we unconsciously accepted this great truth, and from beyond the grave the departed were delivered to us to cherish in all his heavenly beauty.

Ye make no mistake, ye tender mourners, when ye idealize and shed a halo around that dear member of the household circle who has gone to the great home above. He is so delivered to you that you may love him with the full, unselfish love that forgets his human taint and sees him as he is, accepted in the Beloved.

As you see him now, so should you strive to be. You have had your pattern delivered to you from heaven, where you believe him to be like his Lord, for he sees Him as He is!

Foreshadow in your relation to your living friends the love you now feel towards him whom the Lord has accepted. They too are the children of God, but not yet perfected, lifted above the struggles and temptations of this lower life. See them, judge them, help them, forgive them, as pilgrims towards heaven, though they have not yet laid down the staff or exchanged the cross for the crown.

All who are spared to you are delivered to you, as it were, beside the bier of the departed, to be as tenderly ministered to as you would minister to him now if he were raised from the dead. They are delivered to you to have their failings as patiently borne with, their trespasses as freely forgiven, their affection as tenderly fostered and returned.

It is a tendency of the mourning heart to glorify the lost at the expense of the living, encompassed here below with sin and temptation. Rather let your love be increased towards those who are still left in life's rugged way. The word comes to you, "Weep not," or at least let not your tears be a veil between you and the friends still spared to you. Serve them with a new love, labor for them with a new gladness. Be to them a joy in all daily intercourse. Give yourselves to them anew as a companion sanctified by sorrow, to be more loving and forbearing and unselfish, more fitted to help them towards the home in which the loved and lost will be met again in glory.

Nor are you to lack in this new nearness and devotedness to the dear friends that are left you the companionship of the loved and lost. He whom you call dead is now first truly living. He is now brought nearer to you, in a way, than ever before. There is a fresh, sure, firm bond between you. You are perhaps loosely, falteringly clasping the hand of the Lord here on earth. Think of that Lord as holding with the other hand the sainted one who has just come into the Heavenly Kingdom to walk with Him in white beside the river of the water of life.

Christ joins you. You speak to the Master, the Master speaks to him who has entered into his rest. The Lord sees alike your tears and his joy. The Master holds you both in His loving keeping, — you for a while here a cross-bearing pilgrim, your loved one a sainted companion of God and the holy angels.

Live near to the Conqueror of Death, who has the ransomed in His keeping. Weep not. Be patient and hopeful and active and pure, and in a few short days you too will have crossed the dark river. Perhaps even now its waters are rolling at your feet, and bright angels are tuning their harps to give you a song of welcome to the land where the loved and lost are with the Lord in glory.

## IX.

## SELF-DENIAL.

*I will not send them away fasting, lest they faint by the way.* — MATT. xx. 21.

OUR Saviour knew what it was to fast. His fast was a strong expression of His determination to fulfil all duty, as well as to honor every outward form wisely appointed for the good of man. There would be among His followers individuals who must fairly crucify the flesh before they could be penetrated by the life of the soul. To such He would give an example of a triumph over the ordinary needs of human nature, through a struggle with its importunate cravings, a resistance even "unto blood." To each of us practically He so gives a timely warning to keep the body in subjection by any and all means.

Have we not, too, a word here specially to the Christian himself free from all temptation to drunkenness? May not the self-denial of one strong through the habitual control of the body, be a help to the weaker brother who feels within himself an inborn craving that may lead to a destroying habit of vice? When more established Christians are willing to forego the pleasures and elegancies and social amenities of wine at their feasts, or the stronger drinks at entertainments among men, it will be easier for the struggling brother, whose *one* indulgence may be the backward, downward step to a disgraceful fall, and a hopeless return to a career of sin and shame! When there are hosts of refined and self-controlled men and women and boys and girls who dare to say, "I am for total abstinence," the tempted will more easily do likewise! How many a youth after a first carouse, a first humiliation through intoxication, would promptly resolve never again to touch the dangerous cup if sustained by public opinion and a large mass of consistent Christians, above all suspicion of a tendency to sink into a drunkard's grave. Who will set his face and his example deliberately against the practices that lead to the vice that fills our prisons, our insane asylums, and our almshouses, — a vice that destroys the brain of the thinker, robs the workman's arm of its strength, and brings poverty and sorrow and shame into thousands of homes?

Our Saviour knew what hunger was as few ever can know it; He felt a tender compassion towards those who to any extent suffered its gnawing pain. His miracles were not idle exhibitions of power. His touch was to help or to heal. His multiplying of the loaves and fishes seems to have sprung as well from His true compassion as from His willingness to prove that He himself, the Bread from Heaven, was willing giver of daily bread to the needy.

It was His tender mercy, too, to show plainly that sources most insignificant could, at His command, be sufficient for great things.

What cheer these marvellous loaves bring to the anxious heads of families, who cast a dreary look towards the unpromising future, and can only lift up in prayer helpless hands that have craved in vain honest work! For strong and busy hands, with only the prospect of an inadequate result from their untiring efforts, there is a voice of comfort. Your humble labors may be blessed a hundredfold! Your little store, your small success, may be so increased as to keep the "wolf from the door." Fear not! Trust in the Great Giver of Bread.

There are persons who have been willing to take a certain number of days in the year for self-denial, in imitation of the example of Christ, after which time of seclusion and abstinence they have been ready to return with new zest to their ordinary life of pleasure and self-indulgence. This may be a useful exercise, but it is not a faithful following of the Elder Brother. His sacrifice once offered began before His birth with the "Lo, I come!" and found its climax at the death on the cross. It is written even now, He "maketh intercession for us," His lost, wandering brethren.

Let us not consider that our self-denial, that any form of self-denial, can be accepted as our finished work. We are to make an offering day by day and hour by hour, through forgetfulness of self, and loving fulfilment of distasteful duties. We must deny ourselves and take up our cross daily, not merely at an appointed season, or on some great anniversary set apart for specially solemn observance.

We perhaps shrink from the thought of this lifelong self-denial. How consoling to us in this prospect are the precious words, "I have compassion on the multitude; I will not send them away fasting, lest they faint by the way!"

We have no hard task-master, no Pharaoh to wring the utmost from toiling Israel! Our Lord, as a tender Elder Brother, would lay no too heavy burdens on the little ones. He appoints our sacrifices and our pains in a spirit of love. He would discipline and strengthen us and prepare us for nobler and nobler effort. He is ready to help when the way is hard and the courage sinks and the load is intolerable. We do not labor and bear and struggle alone. He, the Great Cross-bearer, is among us and with us. "My Father worketh hitherto and I work" is still the gracious word of our Lord. We are working together with Him for our salvation and the rescue and the joy of our suffering brethren on earth. Fear not that ye shall faint by the way! Ye shall rather come off "conquerors through Him who hath loved" you!

# X.

## ECONOMY.

*Gather up the fragments that remain, that nothing may be lost.* — JOHN vi. 12.

ECONOMY is generally considered as only a suitable virtue for persons of narrow means. For the rich to economize is reckoned a littleness and almost a shame. "Let them that have much spend freely and even lavishly if they will!" says the popular voice.

He who makes the bountiful grain to clothe the fruitful fields, He who could say, "The cattle on a thousand hills are mine," the Munificent Giver of all things, could yet, when clothed in human form, issue the unexpected and homely command, "Gather up the fragments that remain, that nothing may be lost."

The universal neatness of the provisions of nature might lead us to think it possible that the Author of nature would unwillingly see the lone place where flower and bee had kept company marred by the traces of the hasty meal of a great multitude. There is, however, added the full reason of the command: "Gather up the fragments that remain, *that nothing may be lost!*"

The lavish multiplication of the loaves by the hand of the Lord was to give an abundance to the hungry multitude. He is no churlish giver to dole out His benefits with a sparing hand!

Yet the twelve baskets full of fragments that remained must not be lost. They must be carefully gathered, for no good gift should be wasted. We know not what homes were to be gladdened by these remains of the feast. Our Lord knew what humble households would feed on the plenty He had supplied. He knows where to send succor in time of need.

The poor must economize if they would not shiver or starve. Persons of moderate means are prompted to this prosaic virtue by the desire for more elegance or comfort, or for a provision for sickness or old age, or for the great pleasure of giving. To the rich comes the special privilege of economizing as faithful followers of our Lord. They must save, not waste, that they may devote as much as possible of their superfluous abundance to make comfortable and happy and good the suffering brethren of the Master.

Few, even among the very rich, would willingly cast out wantonly as worthless a wholesome loaf of bread, or a basket of luscious fruit, or the sheaves of grain fresh from the hand of the reaper. Yet how many thoughtlessly lavish in worthless trifles or profitless expenses the money that would supply food for a hungry child, or light the dark hovel or kindle the cheerful fire in the desolate home! Call the little sums you throw away so recklessly nourishing rolls for starving children, or refreshing fruits for the stinted invalid. Think of the gratification of your expensive, fickle whims as the rent paid down for the houseless, or work given to the hands that can find no lawful labor to save them from the shame of being stretched out to beg. This will help you to practise economy.

You may say you do give. Very possibly. You may give willingly and abundantly, but while you spend thoughtlessly, lavishly, and wastefully, you could give more, you are robbing the Lord's poor! Use what you have carefully; use it methodically, use it knowing and registering the channels into which your expenditures find their way! You are but a steward. You must one day give an account of your stewardship!

When you save, when you gather up the fragments, give what you save. This is a wise warning for the prosperous. This is the full safeguard against the degeneration of the rich man's economy into meanness or avarice. Give what you can properly spare, is the word for persons of more moderate means. Economy is the duty of all! For the lack of this modest virtue many a home is made comfortless, many a family houseless at last. Make it your duty before God to use the means He has given you, in the constant remembrance that He is the Great Householder whom you serve!

When you save, when you gather up the fragments, see that *nothing* is lost. These are the days when by the ingenuity and charity of man the fragments are carefully utilized. See that nothing is wasted in your house, your office, your workshop, that could do somebody good, that could be transformed or combined or purified so as to be a blessing to the needy!

But there are fragments not of the nature of loaves or fishes or any material thing. There are fragments of time to be caught up and made useful. It has been practically proved that one may learn a new language by employing for a year the odd moments of waiting or idling or dawdling. By care and conscientious watchfulness you can learn and practise the language of prayer, on what you call your most busy days, and have times for meditation that will keep your eyes open to the spiritual world that is ever about you.

Do not sit down in despair in the midst of your broken fortunes. Gather up the fragments cheerfully, and begin again, like the disturbed bird, who lays straw by straw for a new home, singing as gladly as when he made the pretty nest that wantonness has destroyed. Begin again in a better spirit than before, trusting to God for a blessing. Let your foundation be on the rock Christ Jesus, and your watchword, "As for me and my house, we will serve the Lord!"

Gather up the fragments after illness. You may not be what you have been, but you are still an instrument for the service of God and your fellows, — an instrument perhaps polished and sharpened by the illness that has sapped your once prided bodily strength.

Gather up the fragments in old age! You have not long to tarry here. Use your time and powers and prayers lovingly, wisely, gladly, and you may yet while you sojourn below be a joy and a blessing.

We are all poor fragments, unseemly bits, to be fitted together to make a great building, the temple of the Lord, His church, in which He is pleased to dwell now, and which He will glorify hereafter. Let us see to it that we have no unnecessary irregularity of form, no queer, ragged corners about us, that will not fit into the stones beside us. Let us submit to be hewn, if necessary, to suit our proper place, and be contented with that place however small and inconspicuous it may be. There will be a day when our Lord will himself gather up these poor human fragments, the scattered members of His Church on earth, and make them precious stones in the new Jerusalem.

## XI.

## OPPOSITION.

*Neither did His brethren believe on Him.* — JOHN vii. 5.

IT seems strange that any kinsmen or friends, who had watched the youth of the blameless Jesus, could have doubted His divine mission. Their very familiarity with His daily life probably blinded their eyes to His superhuman character. It was hard for them to believe that He who had simply and humbly mixed in the ordinary interests and occupations of the carpenter's home could be the Messiah promised for ages to chosen Israel.

There is ever an unwillingness to acknowledge the greatness that springs up at our side, and, as it seems, might as well have been our own as our more gifted brother's. With this doubt of their powers in their home, in their native city, in their fatherland, the great and good of all ages have had to contend. There is everywhere a strong prejudice against the homespun. The foreign stamp on a fabric makes it more eagerly sought, be that fabric no better, or even worse, than that woven by busy looms almost within our own hearing.

How often some far-seeing scientist or discoverer or writer has failed to be appreciated at home, until some people of another tongue have sealed his claims to celebrity! How often the forerunner of some large enterprise or some needed reform has been greeted with the cry, "Behold, this dreamer cometh!"

The brethren of our Lord were not found among His first eager advocates, but we do not hear that His mother ever swerved from her deep conviction that a great destiny awaited Him. She was even too eager at Cana to have her son show the wonderful power that she was sure was indwelling with Him beside His loveliness and humility.

How many a mother has so trusted her richly endowed son, and waited patiently for his hour of public acknowledgment! And how many such sons have been first fashioned by such a mother's careful training, and been cheered by her affectionate confidence!

That the man Christ Jesus suffered from the doubt and disbelief by which He was met where He had a right to expect trust and allegiance, we cannot question. So He was a sharer in the sufferings of all who follow the lonely path of pioneers in great and blessed works, and are scoffed at by their brethren as wild fanatics who would draw men from the old highroads that have been good enough for their honored fathers.

Be not discouraged, faithful struggler for some great truth, or eager worker for some effort to lift up the fallen or succor the lowly. There is One who understands you and will crown at last your humble labors with abundant success! It may be that here on earth you will never see your finished work. Be not cast down. Good done is never lost. If you but lay a strong foundation, the towers of some great and beautiful and beneficent edifice may lift themselves towards the approving skies when your body has been laid in the dust and your soul has gone to its account!

Alas! there are many who claim that they are misunderstood and unappreciated, when they are chiefly laboring for their own advancement, and seeking for themselves the honor of men. There is One who fully understands them. He reads the self-seeking that mingles with their best efforts. He knows, too, perhaps, that, in spite of this imperfection, they fervently desire to be of use in their day and generation. That Great Master will doubtless cast stumbling-blocks in their way, and surround them with discouragements till their motives are purified and they are made fit to be leaders in a good cause. Work on, tired laborers, bold reformers, but work as the humble servants of the Most High, and you will be less sensitive as to the opinion of men! Seek the success of your noble cause, and not your own honor! Be satisfied if good be accomplished, if that be as the strong fortress on the rocky headland, while your name is but written in the wave-washed sand at its feet!

## XII.

### DEFORMITY.

*Master, who did sin, this man or his parents, that he was born blind?* — JOHN ix. 2.

*Neither hath this man sinned nor his parents, but that the works of God should be manifested in him.* — JOHN ix. 3.

WE hear much complaint about the existing unequal distribution of worldly goods. The possibility of a fair division of property by the State among its citizens is eagerly discussed. Could this be done, the greatest inequalities, and those that are the source of the most unhappiness, would still remain. Were there a certain standard of income to be doled out to all, the thrifty would soon surround themselves with added comfort; the liberal and hospitable would have cheery homes, a source of pleasure to others as well as themselves; the loving would give love and win love; the virtuous would have their peace of mind, the true Christian his Heavenly Father and his home beyond the grave. The careless and idle would soon live in disorder and squalor; the miser would be miserable in the midst of his gold; the cold and selfish would be lonely and deserted; the vicious would be tormented in mind and body; the unbeliever would moan in his secret anguish, "There is no God!"

Nor would the inequality end here. The beautiful would still be beautiful, and the ugly ugly. The old must content themselves with gray hairs and declining powers, while the young man would rejoice in his youth. The gifted would have the pleasure of using his great powers and winning the enthusiastic admiration of his fellows, while the stupid must mope in his dulness, and the silly be the object of contempt.

There would still be the house of mourning and the house of feasting. There would be the glad family circle, and the lone mortal shut out from the voices of childhood and with no loving hand to smooth his dying pillow.

The State could not make "the lame man to leap as a hart," or give eyes to the blind. The State could not make the deaf to hear or the dumb to speak. The State could not give to the giant or the dwarf the ordinary stature of man, or change the negro's swarthy skin. The State could not ordain that in any city "the inhabitant should no more say, I am sick," or that the hungry grave should cease to claim its victims.

There is a natural rebellion in the human heart against poverty and sickness and sorrow and personal misfortune. There is an indignant desire in outsiders to lay the blame of these drawbacks to human happiness on some shortcomings of the sufferers themselves or of their ancestors immediate or remote.

Perhaps there is no kind of misfortune to which it is more difficult to submit meekly than to personal defects or deformity, none under which there is cherished a more bitter and discontented spirit. "What have I done that I should be so afflicted?" is the involuntary question of the sufferer. "Who did sin, this man or his parents?" asks the observer, from the superior point of view of his own perfections.

The majority of the inequalities of life are dispensed by the mighty Creator. He knows where to place the soul here below, and with what body it should be clothed. Of this great school He is the All-wise Master. He orders the discipline and instruction as may suit His varied pupils. A profound belief in His love and wisdom can make the most stiff and stubborn bow cheerfully to His mysterious decrees.

For those children of the Heavenly Father who have received some bodily blemish or defect as their portion, there is a special comfort in the answer given by our Saviour to the question addressed to Him with regard to the man born blind: "Neither hath this man sinned nor his parents, *but that the works of God should be manifested in him."*

Perhaps the world has never seen more marked instances of the triumph of the soul, and its assertion of its superiority over the body, than in the cases of some noble beings afflicted with a personal deformity. Who has not stored in mind as a treasure the remembrance of great, soulful eyes, lighting the face and telling of the conquest of the spirit, in a dwarfed and humpbacked body? Who has not watched the countenance, when the lips were doomed to silence, and the ear to stillness, to see it light with love and friendliness or glow with deep devotion to the Heavenly King. Here is a great and special privilege of personal deformity! It is possible by divine grace so to accept this outer misfortune that the spirit within may be truly sanctified, and honored to manifest that great work of God, the triumph of a loving faith through the unchanging days of a lifelong affliction.

A misfortune outside of one's personality may be modified by time, or forgotten temporarily in some strong, absorbing interest. The lame man, though, must wake every morning to his lameness, the blind to his blindness. These are not misfortunes to be thrown off at will. There is no let-up with them. There is no vacation in the school in which they are the teachers!

## MINISTERING.

Blessed are they who can so take personal deformity or defects that they can make them minister to the glory of Him who can make the blind to see the light of His countenance, and the deaf in their solemn stillness to hear His voice.

For these forms of affliction our Lord Jesus seems to have had a peculiar tenderness. His all-seeing eye could note each secret thought of morbid anguish or swelling bitterness hidden from mortal view. His hand delighted to give to such sufferers the sudden joy of a full and perfect cure. His sympathy is the same now. He will not probably remove the trial, but He can make it cease to be a source of cruel pain, through the sweet submission of a heart that bows lovingly to His sovereign will. He can open the eyes to the shortness of this earthly career, and the little consequence of the outward form of this passing tenement of a soul that is to be glad with Him forever. He can so sanctify and beautify that soul here below as to compel for it reverence and love, even from the little reverent and the little loving. The dweller in a body imperfect or deformed has often candidly said, "I count my misfortune as nothing, wrapped around as I am by love, and convinced as I am that I could not be happier if I had the most perfect body in the world." In such joy and peace the work of God is surely manifest.

With what thoughtfulness and love and tenderness the sound in body should meet the sufferers under personal misfortune! The right-minded must feel the blood boil, and the flush of righteous indignation crimson the cheek, when so-called Christians, — men, women, or children, — can presume to taunt the deformed with their misfortune, or treat them with contempt in consequence of it, or in their absence make it a subject of ridicule or mimicry, or give it a pity which is akin to disdain. Loving tenderness is due to him whom the hand of the Lord has touched.

## XIII.

### PARENTS.

*Lord, have mercy on my son.* — MATT. xvii. 15.
*And his child was cured from that very hour.* — *Ib.* 18.

IT is not strange that our Lord, with His deep appreciation of the sacred ties of family and friendship, should have encouraged their natural consequence, intercessory prayer. Those whom we love we so naturally pray for that in all languages invocations of blessing have become a part of common speech, though sometimes so changed and distorted by thoughtless use that only the philologist can recognize them. To the Christian, however, the "God be with you!" lingers in the "Good-by!" as in the "Adieu!" A large proportion of the miracles of our Saviour were performed in answer to the earnest petitions of the friends of the sick and suffering, often themselves beyond the power of even seeking the help of the Great Deliverer.

Our Lord, too, here as ever, goes before us in the path we should follow. What a treasure we have in His great intercessory prayer! What a comfort to know that we were remembered in that prayer! "Neither pray I for these alone, but for them also who shall believe on me through their word!" Not alone could our Elder Brother pray for them who loved Him. Even for His enemies we hear from the cross the strong cry, "Father, forgive them; they know not what they do!"

Thus encouraged, we may come humbly but confidently to the Lord, with our own eager, importunate prayers, for our friends, for the sick, the sinful, and the sorrowing, adding always the submissive "Thy will be done!"

It is with leaps of heart that we remember that He who is the source of bodily help is likewise mighty for the renewing and sanctifying of the soul. But for this strong assurance, how often Christian parents would be driven to despair! They feel that they themselves are like their own children in the care of their little gardens, who with tiny rake and spade can smooth the ground and with busy feet tread down the narrow paths. They can even root out the springing weeds, but until they lift up their faces to the father with the trustful words, "We are ready now; may we have the seeds?" their work has been at the best but a work of preparation, which without help would have no satisfactory result.

## MINISTERING.

In Christian education the ground must be made ready. Good habits must be formed by precept and example. Special faults must be worked against, and, if possible, early eradicated. A reverence for holy things must be instilled and cultivated. The love of God must be set forth as a natural and joyous tribute to the Creator and Redeemer. All this must be done, but the Christian parent sees that it is but preparing the ground for the seed, — that something which is the beginning of a religious life, through which the child, consciously or unconsciously, gives in its allegiance to God, turns to Him in love, and desires to live according to His perfect law. For this we can pray with the hearty and sincere addition, "Thy will be done!" for is it not written, "It is not the will of your Heavenly Father that one of these little ones should perish"?

Here we have a strong stay! Let us come "boldly to the throne of grace," sure that the fervent prayer of a Christian parent "availeth much!" Such sincere, persistent, believing prayers must eventually prevail! These are the prayers that follow the prodigal to the far country, and bring him home repentant. These are the prayers that may even be powerful for the rescue of the dying sinner. No human messenger may come to tell of repentant last words, but the parent who has been instant in prayer for a wandering child may take comfort in the remembrance of the strengthening words, "If ye shall ask anything in my name, I will do it."

The stronger our interest or real affection for the child, the parent, the brother, the friend, the pupil, the servant, the stumbling, the fallen, the more sure we may be that our prayers for them will be frequent and earnest. Love is the great power for good here, as everywhere. Those whom we truly love we pray for.

Let us never say, "I can do nothing in this world!" The old, the sick, the little child can bring down a blessing on beloved ones, on the family, on the friends, on the native land, on the far heathen! Pray! Pray without ceasing, and many in answer to your prayers shall enter into the Kingdom of Heaven!

# XIV.

## SEEMING DEATH.

*He is dead.* — MARK ix. 26.

ONLY He who is the fount and source of life can certainly know that life in a human being is extinct. The seemingly dead have been resuscitated, and even the supposed coffined corpse has awakened to begin anew the struggle here below. Where to mortal view there is only hopeless death God may see a secret living germ, that is yet to rally and be developed in new and wonderful power.

The child who after our Lord's transfiguration was brought to Him to be cured fell senseless, in one of the paroxysms of his mysterious disease. The murmur "He is dead!" was heard from the solemnized crowd. The disciples had tried in vain on the writhing patient their powers of healing. The father had brought his son to Jesus in a weak faith that uttered itself in the words, "If thou *canst* do anything, have compassion on us and help us!" In the deep desire to have that faith strengthened, he cried out with tears, "Lord, I believe; help thou mine unbelief!" Such a petitioner could never be sent empty away. The child might lie as one dead, but the Lord and Giver of Life was present, and the Angel of Death must fold his wings and yield up his victim.

There is a death when the full pulses beat and the knit muscles are strong for action. Throbbing with life, in the vigor of his manhood, a human being may be "dead in trespasses and sins!" Yet how can we, fellow-sinners, know when that awful point is reached when up in heaven the angels sorrowfully whisper of one to whom they would gladly minister, "He is dead"?

Of this we may be confident, we need not despair of any soul while it is yet in the body. It may yet be awakened, transformed, and sanctified by the same power that has plucked us "as brands from the burning."

We go out generally to seek the sheep that are going astray. Our Saviour "came to seek and to save them that were *lost!*"

It is not uncommon to hear individual children spoken of (sometimes even those growing up in respectable families) as if they were already abandoned criminals, beyond the hope of reform. All physicians express their wonder at the vital power in a child and even a young infant, which enables it to struggle through protracted, dangerous, and wasting disease. The little patient ordinarily recovers from its illness to a joyous and healthy life. The child-invalids, thank God! are few.

There seems to be the same tension, so to speak, in the souls of children. All efforts for the rescue of street waifs have an astonishing amount of success, considering the material presented to be acted upon. The mothers and relatives and teachers who fold their hands in despair and give up the hope of reforming the youthful culprit, the son, the daughter, the nephew, the pupil, who has shown a persistent inclination to go wrong, should think of the love and patience and faith of the true philanthropists who seek out the little ones of the scum of the city, and train them up to be, if not always faithful Christians, for the most part honorable, useful citizens, redeemed from a career of vice, the poorhouse, the prison, or a felon's death!

Never despair in working for children, though there may seem to be a hardness that nothing can melt. Love and happiness and prayer and wise discipline may yet do their blessed work, and the Great Friend of the erring will rejoice over every little one sought out and saved.

Never despair of the reformation of the most abandoned sinner. He has been a babe, a child.

He too had a mother. He has a soul, he has a heart. Pray and hope and labor for him and with him. Conversion is a supernatural thing. The wonder may yet be worked in his dead soul.

There are times in life when one is tempted to pronounce on one's own past personality, "It is dead!" Great affliction may so transform and benumb the whole being that the mourner feels himself dead to all previous interests, and even lifeless and loveless towards the friends who have been next to the dear one who has been snatched away.

Think not, say not, in your sorrow, that you are dead henceforward to life and love! Turn to the Master! He can wake you from this seeming death. He has work for you to do. It may be well that you are somewhat weaned from the too absorbing interests of the past. Bestir yourself for the happiness of the friends still left to you, and the warm currents of old affection will spring up anew within you. Be willing to live, altered it may be, but not dead, rather more truly living, and better fitted to serve the Heavenly King.

But another, a mourner over an inner sorrow, cries out in anguish, "It is my spiritual life that is dead! What I delighted in once, is distasteful to me now. I see, I feel nothing but dulness and deadness and indifference. Old sins are creeping over me, coiling around me. I am helpless! I am dead!"

You are not hopelessly dead while Jesus still lives, if you will but turn unto Him. Cease to examine your own symptoms morbidly, almost willingly dwelling in darkness! Come to the love that waits to receive you! For such as you the Saviour came. He bears the lost sheep home on His loving breast. He suffered that such as you might look and be forgiven. He is the Resurrection and the Life!

## XV.

## THE NURSERY.

*Whoso receiveth one such little child in my name receiveth me.* — MATT. xviii. 4.

MANY a busy mother, shut off from the house of God, and finding it hard to claim a few moments in the hurried day for private prayer, would perhaps be astonished to know how she is regarded in heaven. To the already, in the opinion of outsiders, over-full home she has lately welcomed the little babe she so tenderly clasps in her arms, with the Benjamin portion of love that was awaiting him. He is even more precious than her first darling, received in her untried and undisciplined youth. Then it was often hard for her to be shut up to the duties of the mother, for months deprived from mingling with outward society and enjoying the innocent pleasures that had been so much to her in her girlhood. She was almost afraid, too, of the helpless creature in her inexperienced arms. His every expression of discomfort, she feared, foreboded ill, or was the result of her own unwise treatment. Many tears she shed in secret, to be so transformed from the free glad being of her untrammelled youth. She almost suspected that not even her devoted husband appreciated the sacrifice she was making. Now self is dead within her, and maternal love has its sweet triumph. Such love has its own reward in the tender joy with which she presses this last best gift to her motherly heart. She has received her little one in Jesus' name, and she means to rear him faithfully as a child of God. He has brought her a new blessing from Heaven!

The Christian nursery-maid is doubtless honored with the approving smile of the Master. She looks upon the little ones confided to her care as given her by the Lord, to watch over for His sake. She wraps them round with tender, conscientious care, as ever in the presence of the Lord Christ. She gives them the cheerful sunshine of an affectionate, contented spirit. She folds their little hands in prayer, she answers their crude questioning with the wisdom that comes from above. She leads them to look up lovingly to the Good Shepherd. She feeds His lambs, and is herself abundantly fed of Him. The aged Lord Shaftesbury liked to acknowledge that he owed his lifelong interest in active benevolence to the influence of a nursery-maid, whom he never saw after he was seven years of age.

She passed into the heavenly kingdom or into some other home to sow her seed, but her work in the heart of her little charge was to be for more than an ordinary lifetime a blessing to many of Christ's suffering and wandering children. Lo! the nurses who receive little ones in Jesus' name are indeed receiving Him! They bless and are blessed!

How many Christians who could welcome to their homes little children in the name of Christ trifle away their lives in objectless dawdling or belittling diversions! How many a lonely woman lavishes her affectionate care on some four-footed pet, while in her neighborhood little pairs of human feet are starting helpless on their earthly pilgrimage, to be bruised by the way, or to wander in desolate paths ending in the downward road of open sin. Ye mourners, shutting yourselves up to uncomforted sorrow, ye lonely women who crave something to love, take one little one in Jesus' name! Rescue it from want and sin, and lead it tenderly in the heavenly way! If you cannot have such a child in your own home, find some upright, honest family who will do the work for you for a fair compensation. See your little charge often, love it, and surely new joy will fill your heart, something of the gladness and peace that must come to all who receive a little child in the name of Christ.

# XVI.

## THE CAPITAL.

*He beheld the city and wept over it.* — LUKE xix. 41.

THE capital city is ever the type and representative of the whole nation. Here all that is best and all that is worst are usually found centred. Here we find the most culture and refinement and magnificence. Here dwell the gifted men, the ruling spirits, and the head of the government, crowned or uncrowned. Here are the splendid buildings and the treasures of art. Here are the great benevolent institutions and the organized efforts for the poor and erring. Here are the large givers and the devoted workers. Here are the great churches and the eloquent preachers.

In the capital city, alas! sin stands forward unblushing. Here we have masses of human beings living more like beasts than men. Here we have want and squalor and crime. Here we have the human heart more cold and fierce than the tiger's, sometimes through the selfishness of unlimited prosperity, sometimes through the hard experiences of bitter need. Here we have monster frauds and evil living in high places. Here we have drunkenness in the midst of splendor. Here we have great names and long purses silencing the voice of public indignation. Here we must have the strong military force to keep down the possible mob, the great hospitals to receive the many sick, the giant prisons to shut out from society the criminals it nurtures in its midst. All this, too, in Christian countries! We hide our faces for very shame!

Nor can the quiet dwellers in country places stand in conscious innocence and cast the stones of condemnation on the citizens of a great metropolis. Whose children are they who build up the city and keep it full with their annual influx? Whence came that man whom high position could not keep from crime? "From my home!" says some aged owner of a beautiful rural home, where nature is developed to the utmost beauty, but the God of nature is forgotten. Whose son was it who last entered that prison door a condemned criminal? "My son!" cries the hard-handed peasant, in whose cottage the voice of prayer was never heard, and where riches were counted the highest earthly blessing. The nation cannot cast off the shame of the deeds of its capital city, which is but a concentrated development of itself!

In common parlance the city comes to be a synonym for folly, extravagance, and temptation. "What became of that young man?" we ask. "He went up to the city!" is the answer, and the shrug tells the story of temptation and fall. "Where is that pretty young country girl?" is the question. "She went up to the city!" is the whispered reply, and pity and modesty draw a veil over her end.

Not the city alone is responsible for the degradation that too often overtakes the eager youth or the adventurous girl who cannot be contented in a cottage or a country town. The false standard in the homes from which these young people come, the false view as to what is allowable and most desirable, blights the tender blossom before it is borne within the city gates to wither and die. The lads and unformed girls who go out from Christian country homes in which wealth and worldly honor are counted as nothing in comparison with purity, honesty, and godliness come to the city like the pure water from the mountain lake, that winds its way to house and hearth to refresh and invigorate and keep life in the dwellers in the crowded metropolis. Ye country fathers and mothers, so train your families that they may go to the city as fearlessly as the missionary who trusts himself in a heathen land, to lead like him a faithful, useful, Heaven-blessed and Heaven-rewarded life!

Let every Christian home, high or low, in the great city be a centre of virtue and holy example, and the young from the free country life may safely venture within its bounds, to live and labor, and even "come up" to the capital for solemn seasons of worship, as well as to earn daily bread, or win a wise experience, or drink deep of the fountains of knowledge.

The city is but the initial letter of the whole nation's name. It stands for it, whether the nation will or not. If ever there should be a truly God-fearing people, the capital of that nation will be an earthly reflection of the new Jerusalem, and "the Lord God and the Lamb will be the light thereof."

In all countries the capital city is in a measure the centre of interest and population. What Jerusalem was to the Jews we can hardly imagine. Jerusalem was not only the centre of government, but it was the site of the temple of the Most High, and exalted by its holy memories as well as by the nation's historical past. Not the sacred privileges that had been Jerusalem's portion, not its great buildings nor its greater honors, had been able to save the royal city from a city's sins. Its cup was full! The time of retribution was at hand! Its horrible siege and utter destruction were present to the mind of Jesus of Nazareth as its strong towers met His eyes. What wonder that "when He beheld the city, He wept over it." Its certain doom was not to be averted by His suffering without the gates!

How does the same Lord look now upon our cities? — wherever the seething, sinful elements of destruction are underlying the outward pomp and magnificence? He knows when the bubble will burst! He knew when the swelling lava that had smouldered in the volcano's crater should suddenly roll down its sides, not only to destroy the dwellers on its slopes, but to be accompanied by the hot showers that should bury in far-away graves those cities of old in the midst of their luxury and sin. He only knows what is in store for the great sinful cities of our own day!

Individuals make up the population of cities, and give them their character. It is upon the repentance and reformation and godly living of individuals that the fate of each great city depends. This brings an imperative duty as a Christian and a patriot on every citizen of a mighty metropolis, and is a warning for every home protected by municipal law.

The Almighty would have spared Sodom for

the sake of ten righteous men. Repentant Nineveh was freely forgiven. Merciful and full of loving kindness is the Lord of Heaven.

And what are the special sins of the city from which we are to cleanse heart and tongue and daily walk? Like the venomous snakes, it is more simple to name them than to destroy them!

In the city it is easier to "follow the multitude to do evil," harder to dare singly and in singularity always to do right. In the privacy of the crowded dwellings, it is easier to lead an evil life than in the publicity of the rural districts, where neighbor knows neighbor, and one man's business is the business of all. It is only each man's obedience to a conscience enlightened by God's law that can prevent the moral decline of the dwellers in the city's tempting crowd.

It is to the outward advantages of family, wealth, and distinction that the multitudes of the city bow the knee. Has a Christian a right to give his sanction to sin, however honored the name of the offender? Has the Christian a right to reckon the rich righteous because of his money-bags, or to seek gold for himself as the one thing needful? Are fashion and pleasure and praise to be the objects of life and the moulding influences for old and young? Is a man to be an article valued according to its label, not according to its quality?

Has God a different law for a family in a quiet, country home than for the closely packed tenants of the hived palaces of the city? No! is the clear answer of every honest conscience!

Let that conscience rule, by day and by night, in company and alone, and the dweller in the city is as safe as the hermit in his cell. He is safer, for he has a better sphere in which to act out the great law of love! For his own sake, for the sake of his native land, let every dweller in a great city make himself an offering unto the Heavenly King, to live in purity, in charity, in unworldliness, in holiness, in peace!

## XVII.

## WORKMEN.

*I have finished the work Thou gavest me to do.*
JOHN xvii. 4.

THE workmen's question is often called the great question of the day. Taken in its widest sense it certainly is, for it touches the interests of all mankind. All are, or should be, workmen. There is no place for drones in the human hive! We may even with reverence speak of the Creator as the Master Workman, since all things created are the works of His hands. We have, too, our Saviour's words, "My Father worketh hitherto, and I work," as a still further sanction for the dignity of labor.

It is a low view of duty which looks forward to middle life or declining years as a time of full freedom from all care and occupation, a period of which the daily expression may be, "Soul, take thine ease; thou hast much goods laid up for many years!" From another point of consideration we have the same lesson. How often it has been seen that the eager toiler with mind or body, possessing at last what is to him an abundance of worldly goods becomes, in his longed-for time of rest and self-indulgence, a lethargic, a broken-down, a purposeless idler, or a slave to the pampered body, now become a brutal master.

No! .We are not made for perfect rest, but for action, for work!

We cannot always even choose the career for ourselves or our children. Nor have we the wisdom necessary for such a choice, since the future must always be unknown to us. Many a devout mother has set apart her infant for the ministry, and accustomed him from childhood to consider that his destined mission. Such a mother has too frequently lived to see that son performing his priestly functions without the gifts or the graces requisite for the position. Many a man has droned out his life as an unprofitable preacher of the Word, who would have instructed better by a faithful example, his hand on the plough, or guiding or constructing some intricate modern machine. That labor is truly honorable for which the instrument is fitted, and which is done conscientiously, as apportioned by the Great Ruler of all things!

God-granted ability and providential circumstances hedge around most human beings, and shut them up to a certain path. Many a wilful youth fancies himself, at the start, free to choose his own career. He is disappointed here, cut off there, disabled for this, proved incompetent for that, till he finds himself at last at a work he never dreamed of, and perhaps develops gifts and powers of which he himself has been hitherto unconscious.

It is in vain that we imagine that we are misplaced in life, out of our proper sphere, and thus crippled in our exertions and doomed to come short of our proper destiny. We are not put here simply to shine, but to grow nobler and better! And who can say what is of importance in this strange world? One man's neglect of some simple duty, or unfaithfulness in some trifling detail, may be a source of appalling calamity and widespread destruction. On one honest laborer's conscientious work hundreds of human lives depend, on sea or land, in the factory, or in the far journey!

When we are discontented with our work, it is almost always because we are looking forward to a long, weary round of these uncongenial, unimposing duties. How do we know that we have any earthly future? The clock may be ready to sound out the hour for our appointed change. The trifling duty which we are now despising may have a solemn, momentous importance as our last earthly act. When death pronounces our work finished, the awful question will be how that work was done, not how it was regarded in the eyes of men! And if our lives are spared, how do we know that this treadmill round is really before us? It may be that, like the man who is to superintend large mechanical undertakings and must therefore himself learn practically the first humble duties of the workshop, we, too, must begin at the beginning to be able afterwards to lead and command. Be that as it may, it is ours so to labor in our appointed field that we can lay down at last our little sheaf before the Lord of the Harvest, like the faithful reaper, who is no longer a servant but has been accepted as a son!

It may be that in our humble daily work, which we think unworthy of our acquirements or abilities, there is shut up some opportunity of higher usefulness, which in our self-seeking has escaped us. There may be some soul, precious to God, in whose neighborhood we have been placed to be a comfort or stay or guide. There may be some doubter whose eyes we are to open, some timid penitent we should point to the cross, some lost sheep we should tenderly lead home to the peace and security of the fold. It may be that our faithful fulfilment of uncongenial duties is to give a testimony to the power of Christian principle, better than ten sermons. It may be that our struggle to do well where we do not want to be is to strengthen our own tottering religious life, and plant our feet firmly on the Rock of Ages.

Perhaps you have never yet begun your destined, your all-important work, ever to "work out your own salvation with fear and trembling." Perhaps you have never laid the willing hand in those blessed hands that were stretched on the cross that they might lead us to the Heavenly Kingdom.

There has been but one being in human form who could look up to the Father and say, "I have finished the work Thou gavest me to do." We hear often of men cut off in the midst of their labors, leaving in youth or in manhood an unfinished work. So the world speaks, as if alone the sudden close of an earthly career caused the incompleteness of the work. Look at the aged saint who, after a pure outward life and long years of active usefulness, lays down his hoary head in the grave. Does he presume to come before his Heavenly Master as with a finished work? He too must bow down before the throne of the All-Perfect as an unprofitable servant, a helpless sinner, a transgressor of the strict law, a banished dweller in outer darkness, but for the one faultless life, the one all-sufficient sacrifice!

We cannot know the peace of that nature which in the presence of the Omniscient could say, "I have finished the work Thou gavest me to do." Yet we have been brought into brotherhood with the One Perfect Man.

He has owned us in the words, "I go to my Father and your Father, my God and your God!" Through Him we may draw near as welcome sons and daughters of the Lord God Almighty! Our poor deeds shine with a light reflected from Him who is the Light of the World. He has been pleased to choose us as His own, and will gather us at last into His Father's House.

# XVIII.

## CONSTANCY.

*Having loved His own which were in the world, He loved them unto the end.* — JOHN xiii. 1.

THERE is a special sacredness about the last hours of Jesus among His disciples. He, who was the Lord from heaven, humbly ministers to His human followers. Knowing all their stumbling past and their faltering future, He serves them in the fulness of His love, and for a perpetual example to all believers. We behold and wonder and adore.

We may not comment on the condescension of our Master, but we turn towards the daily life that surrounds us, resolved to be more humbly, willingly, unselfishly, and lovingly ready for the modest help we can render to those whom we are bound to succor and cherish. In humility and in constancy we will try to love as our Lord loved, and to minister in the spirit in which He ministered.

Among the most painful of all the vicissitudes that try us here below are perhaps the estrangement and alienation of persons to whom we have been closely allied. This is even not impossible in the tie that is purely voluntary, which we ourselves form as the closest and dearest that earth can know. Where this tie has been formed between Christians who have the deepest congeniality as to the great purpose of life, and its highest aims and hopes and joys, this change is happily rare. The broken engagement is most common where the pair have pledged themselves to each other after trivial intercourse in the midst of giddy pleasure, or for the mere attraction of external charms, or from the mercenary hope of worldly advantage from the connection. Such ties, so lightly formed, are naturally most easily broken. Yet even here the rupture may be to the forsaken one a source of bitter pain. Sometimes, while deep in the shadow of this peculiar trial, there comes a burst of cheering light. The world is for the time thrown into the background. It has proved itself uncertain footing and a poor reliance. In the midst of unreasonable doubts of all earthly affection comes the strong conviction of the constancy of One who, "having loved His own, loved them unto the end." Here is a revelation of enduring joy. Slowly but surely there is an alteration in the whole purpose and tenor of that human life, and the sorrow of youth becomes an inestimable blessing.

Estrangement may happen even after marriage, when before there has been true affection or its deceptive counterfeit. Happy, then, if the joined hands are held together by soft baby fingers clasping them both! Happy if so a common love, a common responsibility links again the hearts that were beginning to cherish mutual animosity and repulsion.

It may be that love languishes in but one of the wedded pair, while with the other it is fresh and strong. Here, with ordinary wisdom and self-control, there is always hope. There is ever in love a mighty power. If that love is stayed on the higher love which beautifies and ennobles the character, in time it is almost sure to win the day. Let the wife, in such a case, never despair, but humbly pray and minister and cherish and wait!

But what if affection has died out on both sides? Here comes in the great word of "duty." Love is but one part, though the great part, in the marriage promise. Duty well done is good ground on which it is even possible for the apparently dead growth of wedded affection to spring to life. Perhaps the two are harsh, unlovely, selfish, low-toned. Let them both, with God's help, try to be all that they should be. Is the bond galling? Death may dissolve it tomorrow! Then how will your reckoning stand before the Heavenly King, who has "set men in families"? How will your reckoning stand for thought and word and deed? The highest form of friendship can never die out, though the friends may be separated by the wide ocean or by the long waves of time. The pen brings heart near to heart, and with perhaps the more openness when the deep-down congeniality is more and more felt as friends are so placed that they cannot share the every-day interests that first helped to unite them. True friendship declines but through the deterioration of character on one or both sides. Increased riches or other worldly advantages may fill one heart with selfish pride. Misfortune may assail the other and open the way for suspiciousness and morbid bitterness. These sad changes must be watched and guarded against by the constant interchange of simple and even humble offices on both sides.

Let the prosperous remember that with his prosperity his intimate friend should be made more comfortable and happy. This need not be done necessarily by direct gifts, but by sharing with an old friend, as far as possible, in a quite natural way the many charms and privileges of a beautiful home and its accessories, and a life free from pressing care.

Let the friend in the shadow of misfortune or limited means remember that he has still earth's best gift to offer, which no money can buy, and no high position can insure, even a true unworldly affection. Attention may be given to outward advantages, but love is a tribute they cannot buy. The prosperous have their times of bitter need. To them sorrow and sickness come as well as to the dwellers in the humblest homes. Then the face of a real friend must be counted by them as an inestimable blessing. There are times of contagious illness in palatial homes, when hired strangers can hardly be procured or trusted in the sick-room. Then only true affection offers its efficient aid. Let friends love unto the end, like the Master, and nourish love by acts of unselfish affection.

Even in families joined by the closest ties of blood hearts may be alienated or grow cold. The little feet that have kept step with each other often take widely diverging paths in life. Jealousy separates brothers and sisters who have knelt at the same mother's knee. A conscientious and habitual effort to be useful to each other, and to lovingly share each other's joys and sorrows, may forestall estrangement and knit more closely the family bond. The simplest means for this purpose should not be despised. A garment made by a sister's hand for the brother's new baby, joy promptly expressed for the success of a sister's boy at school, an invitation to meet an agreeable stranger or to join a choice gathering of friends, may give pleasure, and show the sincere wish to keep old ties strong and childhood's affection unchanged. Frequent letters during times of necessary separation, free, familiar letters, can keep hearts far separated by space very close together. This often costs real self-sacrifice, but it should be perseveringly and conscientiously done, if you would not have your distant brothers and sisters and their families become to you as indifferent strangers.

We may not wash one another's feet in our form of society, but we can strive by kindly offices, humble though they be, to keep near to those whom God has given us, and not only to love them to the end, but to make them feel that we love them, and be the happier for it.

There are times when the strong faults of friends or relatives are forced upon us by circumstances, or moments to them of overpowering temptation. They show themselves in an unlovely light. They are perhaps harsh or selfish or unjust or grasping. We feel a chill creep over our affection, and we nourish a misgiving that they are worse than we had ever dreamed possible. Now is the time to summon to our remembrance the great example of Him who, "having loved His own, loved them unto the end." Now there must be prompt resistance with resolution and prayer, or there will be real alienation from friend or brother. No slights, no suspicions should prompt us to willingly withdraw our loving interest from those who have been bound to us by the ties of friendship or the sacred bonds of a common home!

A widowed mother may find that she is left alone in her old age. She who has been first with her children is now fifth or tenth instead. She is tempted to shrink into herself in a hurt and wounded spirit. Let her rather unselfishly remember that if she were now indispensable to her children, as she was in their youth, she must soon leave them comfortless. That she can be more easily spared is the promise of less sorrow to her sons and daughters. Nor must she believe that her chlidren are really estranged. New duties and new affections have become for the time paramount; but the old love is there, to bloom and blossom and perhaps come to perfection beside her grave. If her love and influence have been worth anything, they will have their softening trace for good, when she lies low in the silent tomb. While she is in the body, let her be ingenious in finding ways of showing thoughtful love to her children, though they may seem to be unmindful of her. She will thus nourish her own best treasure, a heart full of love, and perhaps keep warm their love in return. How precious to the aged mother's heart is the remembrance that the Great Friend, to whom she gave her solemn vows in her girlhood, "loveth His own unto the end." He knows no shadow of change. Let her lean upon Him, and love unto the end, in those declining years of life, when a kind of torpor may creep over the heart, and the affections be chilled in the sombre evening hour. The old must keep up the practice of loving, not sink into a dull, selfish round of little daily comforts and purely personal interests. If they cannot do much for their dear ones, there are still some simple, tender offices to fill. They can have at least the willing ear to hear of others' joys and sorrows, the willing lips to speak sympathy and hope and holy trust, the willing heart, that while it beats can thrill its warm response in the spirit of devoted, unselfish, true affection.

The unutterable love of our Lord for His own is a deep source of consolation in hours of spiritual depression. The Christian pilgrim feels himself sometimes so sinful and unlovely, it is hard for him to believe that man or angel can care for him, much less the high and holy God, who knows exactly what he really is, in spite of his best efforts to be faithful and true and pure. With a rush of joy comes at such an hour the remembrance of the loving ministry of our

Lord to His own, whom "having loved, He loved unto the end." The discouraged pilgrim cries out, "I am of *His own*. He wishes it. I wish it. It is done now, if never before, — His abounding love will accept me, and will sanctify me more and more. He will love me all along my uncertain and perhaps dark and erring future. He will not let me utterly fall. He whose existence is without end will love me evermore!"

## XIX.

## FORGIVENESS.

*Father, forgive them; they know not what they do.*
LUKE xxiii. 34.

HUMAN beings judge others by themselves. Each must apply to all his fellow-creatures his own measure, a measure formed after his own limited experiences, outward and inward. Perhaps unconsciously, poor, short-sighted, sinful man would even judge his Almighty Creator by the low standard of his own heart. It is one of the hardest tasks of the earnest Christian pastor to convince his flock, collectively and singly, of the willingness of God to forgive the sincere penitent at once, wholly, and forever. The conscience-stricken offender will cherish the secret thought that there is some lingering grudge against him, some hidden record of his past misdoings, to be sometime brought forward to his utter condemnation. It is not so that God forgives, for Jesus' sake. Our Lord, by His great sacrifice, has fully redeemed us. He has bought us with a price we cannot estimate. The gold has been paid down that ransoms every atom of the poor dust of the earth, the clay of Adam's race. The love that has bought us was not blind love. Our Lord knew the human heart as no man can know it. He had fathomed it by His divine power. He had companied with weak mortals as His fellows. He had been side by side with them in pain and sorrow and temptation and death. He who could understand the horrible danger and malignity of sin could tenderly plead the ignorance of His enemies, as an excuse for the cruelty and injustice of His deserved death. Let us turn to our fellow-men with the consideration for their shortcomings that we have learned at the cross.

Forgiveness seems to us a passive virtue when we have nothing to forgive; but let us once be really wronged, and the passive virtue forsakes us. Forgiveness is a Christain attainment, and generally developed through struggle and prayer. The clearer the sense of right in the offended one, the more difficult he often finds forgiveness. What perpetrated towards outsiders he would have considered an offence without excuse, rouses his righteous indignation, of course, when he himself is the sufferer, with the added sharpness of the feeling of personal injury. A deep Christian realization of our own position towards our Heavenly Judge, as blind, helpless, and unworthy, should soften our hearts into forgiveness of our erring fellow-creatures.

Much pain is inflicted, much injustice is shown by offenders so absorbed in their own selfish interests, so thoughtless of the claims of others, or so brutally stupid as to what may harass and wound the human beings about them, that they are hardly responsible for the direct injury involuntarily inflicted. They are solemnly responsible for the unloving and unlovely state of mind which makes self and self-indulgence the chief and absorbing interest of life.

It may truly be said of nine tenths of those who pain and wrong their neighbors, "They know not fully what they do." This consideration robs the injustice and unkindness of its personality towards its object, and may help him to feel less resentment towards the offender. The remaining one tenth may be so actuated by wilful malice that the more pain they can inflict the greater their gratification. Such natures, so far degraded, can well call for pity instead of anger. Where the image of God is so defaced, the indignation of the true Christian must ever be tempered by holy sorrow.

In the "short madness" of anger, cruel words may be said that break old bonds and leave wounds that only the Heavenly Hand can heal. The fury passes by with the hot-tempered man. He can hardly remember what he has said in his rage. He wonders that others cannot as easily forget words that he is sure in his calmer moments he could never indorse. Of him whose offence was so committed it may well be said, "he knew not what he did," and his regret and acknowledgment may be frankly accepted. Yet *he* must remember that he is guilty of so indulging his violent temper that he becomes for the time like the irresponsible madman, who may in a wild moment become one of the race of Cain.

When chafing under some supposed injury, some seemingly cruel word that has wounded us to the quick, let us look to it if there be not in us some peculiarity of character, or some cherished sensitiveness or suspiciousness of nature, that may make us susceptible to the slightest appearance of unkindness or lack of consideration as regards our feelings or our claims. The blame may be really in ourselves, rather than in our blundering, tactless companion.

In dealing with children the plea of our Saviour for His murderers should be ever kept in mind. Parents and teachers see often in children faults and sins the dangerous germs of future crime, and feel the same indignation towards the erring child as if he could grasp all the evil that is shut up in his hasty act in a moment of overpowering temptation.

Such sin should be looked at, if possible, as it seems in the eye of the child. He should be tenderly dealt with, though his punishment must be in a measure in proportion to the danger to his own soul and to society from the persistence in the kind of offence of which he has been guilty.

In the haunts of ignorance and vice much that is known as sin in the Christian home has become the natural atmosphere, and offends neither the uncultured taste nor the deadened conscience. This too must be remembered in pitying love, while at the same time it should prompt to a stronger and more sustained effort to open those poor darkened eyes to the beauty of holiness and the only way of happiness and peace.

What can the most advanced Christian know of the real danger and the venomous character of sin? What are our downfalls in the view of a pure and perfect God, or even to the holy angels? We may well be gentle towards all the lost sheep of the Good Shepherd!

It is never to be forgotten that the whole church of Christ must be washed and made clean by the blood of the Lamb before it can be presented before the throne of God, accepted in the Beloved.

## XX.

## TRUST.

*Into Thy hands I commend my spirit.* — Luke xxiii. 40.

THE suspicious despots of old dared not drink of any cup before it had been tasted by some submissive subject. Our Lord and King drank of mankind's most bitter cup that it might be freed from its poison, even for His most humble followers. He tasted death for every man, and robbed it of its terrors. He has shown his brethren in mortal form where to find their trust and help in the dying hour.

How many saints on the verge of glory have echoed the words of the crucified Master, "Father, into thy hands I commend my spirit!" In peace and trust they have passed from earth to heaven.

Why is it that the faith on which alone we can rely for support in our last moments is not summoned to sustain us in the worries and emergencies that throng around our daily path? We seem content to leave the stars in their courses to the care of the great Creator, never fearing that they shall swerve from their appointed round; yet we shrink from wholly confiding the details of our insignificant lot to the ordering of the All-wise. We are too much like the timid woman who, in a moment of sudden danger by the way, snatches the reins, stupidly fancying her weakness and inexperience her best reliance. Why cannot we trust our Heavenly Friend day by day and hour by hour, in the sacred confidence which says sincerely, "Father, into Thy hands I commend my spirit!" It is the spirit for which we fear. We tremble lest it should not have strength to triumph over the bodily pain which threatens us, or to endure the affliction that is hanging over us or the humiliations and mortifications that are in store for us. We fear the temptation that has before mastered us, the doubts that have once desolated our peace, the loss of the consciousness of the presence of God, which is our best treasure. We are harassed by forebodings and distressed by circumstances, instead of quietly, without anxious misgivings, commending the spirit to God, and doing faithfully in simplicity and peace the present duty that is plainly set before us. Here is the secret of calm serenity in the midst of "the chances and changes of this mortal life." This mortal life! That we are mortal, doomed to die, is sometimes the secret source of the gloom that overshadows some sincere but trembling Christian. This may be, though our Lord has Himself descended into the grave that there should be light from the tomb, and hope in the valley of the shadow.

Death is, must be, for the true believer, the rising of the Sun. Not that the physical sun really rises for us, but we are turned so that we see its perpetual shining. So is it with the Sun of Righteousness. He knows no shadow, but the veil of the body hides the fulness of His light from our spiritual vision. Even while yet in the flesh, many devout souls have been able to say in the hour of departure, "Whereas I was blind, now I see." The burst of heavenly glory has reached the dying saint, even before the parting pang. The eye has glowed with rapture, the face has been glorified by a holy light, telling of a foretaste of heavenly joy in the Christian life's triumphant close.

Why should we fancy we have a long journey to take to reach the loving Lord, whom we have believed to be ever at our side, and to whom, in the stillness of the solemn night, we have spoken, in the depths of our spirit, in voiceless prayer? Away with the thought that we are to be suddenly thrust into an unknown and awful presence! "God is Love!" The Lord Jesus is His express image! He with whom we have walked by the way and sat down at meat, He who has been our chosen companion and comfort and refuge all the days of our pilgrimage, will not be suddenly withdrawn from our side. It is the will of the risen Lord that we should be with Him where He is. Of His welcome of indescribable love beyond the bed of death we may be sure. Let us not fear the dying hour, but rather fear anything that may separate us from the present companionship of Him who is the Resurrection and the Life.

There may even be no death awaiting us. The light of the everlasting day may give us a glad surprise, and we may see the Lord coming to claim as His own the most humble of His followers.

How human nature clings to the conviction that death is to be prefaced by some sacred, hallowed time, in which the heart will be purified and prepared for the great change! The common hours of this workaday world are in most cases the only time of preparation for the solemn moment of departure. There is generally an illness, trifling it may be at first, but growing more and more serious, with more and more absorbing pain, or discomfort, or dimness and wandering of mind, and then a short, hurried close, a surprise to the surrounding friends, perhaps, as well as to the patient.

The messenger of death may even come to the strong man in the midst of the struggle of life, and call him at once to an account. A long period of discipline is awarded to some earthly pilgrims, and blessed to open their eyes to holy things and their souls to a personal share in the great salvation. These are exceptions. The Christian's life is the only wise, sure preparation for the Christian's death.

Men would also fancy that some great change is to take place on earth before the second coming of our Lord. *He* tells us that in the midst of the ordinary occupations of life, the round of pleasure or the stir of business, the sudden glory may dawn. When we lie down tranquilly at night we may wake to the coming of the Lord, "with ten thousands of His saints," to reign the King Everlasting.

Can we say from the depths of our heart, "Even so! Come, Lord Jesus!" death has indeed no power over us, for we have already passed from death unto life!

# Crucified.

## CRUCIFIED.

*And sitting down they watched Him there.*
MATT. xxvii. 36.

IT is only a kind of doubt that thrusts its unfeeling hands into the pierced side of our Lord, and puts its curious fingers into the prints of the nails. These sacred wounds are approached with loving awe by the true believer. No human words, no sensational appeal to the feelings, can rightly impress upon us the sufferings of the cruel cross endured for our sake.

We stand silent before the Man of Sorrows, in His hour of deepest humiliation. We bow low before the cross, in humble, voiceless adoration. Its solemn mysteries, that angels desire to look into, are shrouded from our mortal eyes. We can but pray that God will so lift the sacred veil that we may more clearly see and feel the great sacrifice in its loving majesty, and yield in return the grateful, willing obedience of a devoted heart.

Let us read in faith and humility the Gospel account of the close of the finished work of our Lord. Let us strive to remember that those last hours are ever fresh in the memory of the Unchangeable. It is as if He were now willingly offered for us, for the sins of the whole world. So standing beside the cross, may our hearts be moved to new penitence and deeper love.

# Risen.

I. The Grave.
II. In Remembrance.
III. Vision.
IV. By the Way.
V. The Old Testament.
VI. The Sheep.
VII. Daily Bread.

# Risen.

## I.

### THE GRAVE.

*They have taken away my Lord, and I know not where they have laid Him.* — JOHN xx. 13.

HOW often since the weeping Mary uttered the words, "They have taken away my Lord, and I know not where they have laid Him," has the same cry come again from a sorrowing heart! How many Christians have fallen asleep at night in such calm trustfulness, such vivid consciousness of the presence of the Heavenly Friend, that death could hardly have been a more wholly leaving of the soul and body in the hands of the dear Master! Yet, after a night of quiet rest, these very Christians have awakened in such spiritual dulness and dimness that the lonely heart has cried out almost in despair, "They have taken away my Lord, and I know not where they have laid Him!"

How blessed for such mourners is the thought of the resurrection! Jesus is risen once for all.

He is not now merely present for the few followers who could see Him with their mortal eyes, but in every land and in every place. *We* may close our eyes, an unwelcome film of dulness or doubt may shroud them, but He is there, ever present and at our side. He is it not with us only when our souls glow with devotion and we are almost lifted out of the body by the sense of His nearness and abounding love! He is around us and within us in the mists of the early morning, when we, groping, seek Him in our blindness and find Him not. Perhaps He is looking with especial tenderness on His darkened, fumbling children, grieving for the lost joy of the eventide. We may change; our bodily or our spiritual eyes may be open or closed; but the Lord Jesus knows no alteration, no alienation. He is eternally the same.

Let us comfort ourselves with these cheering thoughts on such dreary mornings, and begin anew our daily duties, counting no appointed path too narrow, since there, where He has fashioned our way, we can follow His footsteps in humility and patience and love! We cannot expect to be like the saints in the New Jerusalem, who need no sun nor moon, for the Lord God is their temple and their light. Let us accept gratefully the gleams of heaven that come to brighten our earthly journey, sure that if it be onward and upward, it must end in the perfect day.

Let us not sit weeping at the grave of our lost spiritual joy, perhaps the deep sense of acceptance of our early discipleship. Let us rather turn to the loving Lord at our side, who is leading us, as it seemeth Him best, to His Father and our Father, His God and our God.

Those devoted women who were early at the sepulchre, with the natural longing to do something more for the body of the dear departed, have their kindred spirits in our own days. How our hearts cling even to the poor fleshly tabernacle in which our friend has dwelt! God has wisely doomed that body to a great and awful change. We must put it away from us. Some heathen nations have tried to set this change at defiance; but no voice comes from the dry lips, no light of love brightens the dull features. Were it possible to keep near us the unchanged faces and forms of the dear household companions whose souls are in heaven, how tantalizing, how agonizing, would be that bodily nearness, when hand gave no response to hand, and for the throbbing heart there was no answering throb in the cold, silent corpse! Thanks be unto God, the dead body must be put out of our sight, and our fond hearts can only find their treasure in heaven.

Even Christians will "seek the living among

the dead." How many eyes full of tears look down on the mound where the silent sleeper has been laid, rather than up to the heaven where he is rejoicing! How many mourners willingly linger in the churchyard to indulge and perpetuate their grief! Let them rather accept their affliction, and, leaning on God, who alone can support them, go forward as cheerfully as may be, like penitent, disciplined children who bow to the Father's will!

Yet not even the poor graves of our departed should be neglected. Who would not be pained to hear the name of the departed lightly or disrespectfully mentioned? Who would not be wounded to see his garments, his books, his favorite possessions handled like ordinary things of earth? "The grave is but his wardrobe locked." We know "he is not there." Yet let us pay due respect to the resting-place of the body which has been the dwelling of one who has been dear to us. Let us beautify that last earthly home, if we will; but let us remember "He is not here," is its appropriate inscription.

When we think of our own departure, let it not be with any gloomy associations of the cemetery and the silent tomb. Let us rather look rejoicingly forward to the time when, free from care and temptation, we "shall be ever with the Lord!"

## II.

## IN REMEMBRANCE.

*In remembrance of Me.* — LUKE xxii. 19.

THE thronging cares and pleasures of this life so fill the minds, even of the devout, that it is only by determined effort and something like a fixed routine that they keep the reality of spiritual things frequently and lovingly before them. God, who knows so well our needs, has helped us to a holy order for this sacred purpose.

We have the one day in seven, when the toilers may cease from their weary labors, and the anxious may turn from their necessary thought for the future. The stir of innocent social pleasures is hushed, that the "still small voice" may be heard. A silence steals over the busy, noisy world, and lo! the far-off harmonies of heaven break upon the ear. Sweet Sabbath bells call to the house of prayer, where dull lips and duller hearts are helped to petitions for all the soul and body need. Then a priceless blessing falls on the few gathered together in the humble sanctuary, as well as on the great congregation in the lofty temple.

But there is not alone given the public worship on the Lord's Day as a reminder of holy things and a help in the Christian life. There is the Lord's Supper, — that simple sacrament, adapted to all times and all climates and all peoples, the rich and the poor, the wise and the unlearned, which when devoutly received, in remembrance of the Lord Jesus, brings its deep and special blessing.

For our homes we have the commands, "Search the Scriptures!" and "Pray without ceasing!" We have the closet and the family altar and the grace at table, to give a holy flavor to our food and remind us of the Giver.

Such beneficent landmarks are set up along the path of the pilgrim heavenward, that in the manifold interests of this life he may not forget its object and end. Such an outward framework we have around our inner life. Such a body have we, in which our higher being lives and grows. Such a fair cup is given us from which to taste the healing waters. Landmarks they may be for the blind, — an empty framework, nothing growing in it; a fair cup, the contents untasted; a dead body, quickened by no spirit within!

We may forget God in the midst of the sacred

order of His own planning. He may be remembered only in the dark hours, when some sudden and awful warning reminds us that we must stand at last before the Almighty Judge.

How welcome to the soul is this holy order when there is the true sonship, the devotion to our Lord Jesus, that gladly accepts all aids to His loving remembrance and to the faithful following of His example!

But it is not alone our spiritual duties that are to be done in remembrance of our risen Lord. Not so we cherish the memory of an earthly friend. The slightest wish of the loved and departed has for us the sanctity of law. The simplest act becomes a hallowed pleasure if we can say of it, "So my father wished me to do;" "This my mother taught me;" "To do this reminds me of my sister, my brother." So we feel towards our human friends who have "gone before us."

Let us remember the Lord Jesus more lovingly and constantly; then will His least precept become a cherished treasure. How diligently we should read over and over His sacred words, to see how He would wish us to live and labor and love!

How much would be left undone if we should ask ourselves, "Can I do this in remembrance of my Lord? Can I do it remembering His love for mankind? Can I do it remembering His eye is upon me?"

Let us be living momuments in memory of our Lord, His character, His words written upon us, poor stones of earth, honored to be raised in remembrance of Him!

## III.

## VISION.

*Then were the disciples glad, when they saw the Lord.*
JOHN xx. 20.

HOW often after an ordinary parting between friends, the sudden and unexpected return of the traveller, perhaps for some trifle forgotten, or perhaps for a few more tender words, has lightened to all the pain of separation and given it a milder form.

The parting between our Lord and His disciples was no severing of a common tie. Daily intercourse with a being of a life and character like His must have called out the warmest feeling of which our nature is capable. The adored Master had not been merely taken away by death. The Messiah had suffered a shameful crucifixion amid the revilings of the scoffing crowd. For the resurrection, the disciples, in their blindness, seem not even to have looked. The very women, whose devotedness kept them near their Master through all His last bitter pains, had no thought of meeting Him in the early morning, risen from the dead. What wonder, then, that "the disciples were glad when they saw the Lord," unmistakably living, triumphant over the dark grave?

There are thousands of instances on record where, by the converting grace of God, wanderers in the dreary paths of sin have been suddenly allowed to see with the soul's clear vision the beauty and love of the Lord Jesus, and have been so transported by the sight that they have seemed for the time lifted above the common sorrows of humanity. Not so is the spiritual light generally given to the renewed soul. There are devout men and women who might truly use the words, "When Thou saidst unto me, 'Seek ye My face,' my heart said, 'Thy face, Lord, will I seek;'" yet there has been with them no sudden transition from darkness to light, but a gradual dawning unto the fulness of day.

The child who goes forth in the crowded city to meet his returning father, sees with bounding joy the longed-for form in the distance amid the moving, changing throng. Now he loses him for a moment in this group or that, but still the eager little one presses on. His father once seen, he knows where he is, though he may for an instant be shut out from the loving, seeking eyes. The meeting comes at last, and how pure and full is its joy! Hands are joined, and onward the two together go homeward in sweet communion.

Such even is the experience of some Christian disciples. They are glad, indeed, when they have their first far-away glimpse of the Lord they are seeking. He is not always in sight for them, yet they go on in the path of prayer and duty, now brightened by a clear view of Him who is the Eternal Truth, and now in dimness in the midst of this toiling, changing world. At last they are privileged to feel, as it were, a firm hand clasping theirs, and leading them steadily towards the Better Country. They may not have the brightness of the face of the Lord revealed to them, but they are sure of His holy presence, and walk gratefully towards the Kingdom of Light.

There are other sincere inquirers, who, through some mental or physical peculiarity, or some spiritual discipline of the Great Physician, never seem to find on earth the Lord they are truly seeking. How great must be the joy of such wanderers in this vale of tears, who in a pure practice have sought the Lord, by careful investigation, by loving ministry to their fellows, and by pouring out the soul in prayer, to find His sure promise fulfilled at the gate of heaven, and for the humbled pilgrim the blessed welcome ready, "Enter *thou* into the joy of thy Lord!"

## IV.

## BY THE WAY.

*What manner of communications are these that ye have one to another, as ye walk?* — LUKE xxiv. 17.

HOW naturally we fall into unstudied talk with a friend who draws near to us by the way. He has voluntarily thrown himself into our company, and our heart opens to him. How often a traveller has revealed the secrets of his soul to an attractive stranger, met for the first and perhaps the last time, and yet soon felt to be a fellow-pilgrim to the same Heavenly Home. It is sometimes easier to give such confidence to a stranger than even to the well-known members of the domestic circle. For a person of a reserved nature it is sometimes trying to see daily face to face one to whom the inmost heart has been opened. The stranger who has heard of our trials, our longings, and our aspirations, goes his way, and we see him no more till we stand together before the "great white throne." Men, ill at ease in a godless life, have laid bare their souls' secrets to a devout fellow-traveller, and in that one interview the good seed has been sown to spring up and bear fruit for the far future.

There is something peculiarly friendly and human in the manner in which the risen Lord joined the dejected disciples on the way to Emmaus, and would share their conversation and inquire into their sorrow. With the same loving sympathy He is ever drawing near to us "by the way," whether we are alone or in company. With no human friend at our side, we may often, as we walk, have the sweetest communion with our Elder Brother. No one of the hurrying passers-by may know what manner of conversation we are having by the way, but we may return to our homes, not only refreshed by exercise in the open air, but by converse with the one Heavenly Master.

The Lord is our companion in our walks when forgotten, as well as when remembered. How often He might address to us, in a tone of reproach, the question to the sorrowing disciples. How much foolish talk, gossip, and worse, may be uttered in the secrecy of the public street, or in the silent woods, where eye need not meet eye, and the mouth may be prompt to speak and the ear to listen. It is in these unexpected and unstudied talks that the real person is more surely met than in more conventional intercourse.

The child prattling at the father's side in the open daylight is different from the same child as one of the family group, and often more free and confiding. The father reads deep down in the little heart, and is the better prepared to lead it to the Children's Best Friend.

Turning their backs on the church door, the late subdued listeners start for their homes. Too many Christians act as if their Lord had been shut into the temple behind them, and could no longer hear their words or read their hearts. They who have apparently joined in prayer and praise, they who have listened devoutly to the exhortation, have their thoughts let loose like birds to fly east or west, on a good or an evil errand. Their light, unprofitable talk may dissipate or blot out the good impression made in the church on some unstable soul. How great the responsibility of such careless trifling in the very shadow of the temple of the Most High. Happily there are Christians who leave the house of God deeply solemnized themselves, and unconsciously, by their power of sympathy, or through an unstudied utterance of their own holy thoughts, strengthen the impression for good that has been made on the companion at their side.

Let us not forget that the Lord ever draws near us by the way, and has a share in all our natural talk. Nor need this remembrance make us either gloomy or sanctimonious. He who made the golden sunset, the sparkling water, and the many-hued flowers that gladden us in the open air, would not cloud our cheerfulness, or even check our innocent smiles. He cannot frown on the kindly greeting or the friendly grasp of the hand at the church door, for He is the God of Love.

To mourners and to all the sorrowing comes with peculiar pertinence the Saviour's searching question, "What manner of communications are those that ye have one to another by the way, as ye walk, and *are sad?*" It is not uncommon for the human heart to be full of bitterness in the time of trial, or even of passing depression. The ordinary self-restraint is relaxed, and murmurs and complaints flow spontaneously from the lips. Let such gloomy, desponding talkers fancy the question of the risen Lord addressed to them in gentle reproof. It is in deep affliction that the rounded Christian life gives its best testimony. The hand that on the sunny path has surely clasped the hand of the Son of Man, is tenderly led by Him through the waters of tribulation.

The gentleness of our Saviour's address to the unbelieving and sorrowful disciples should be imitated by us in all our dealings with the afflicted. We need not be chafed by their repinings or their rebellion. Let it be rather our precious privilege to lead them lovingly to the Man of Sorrows. If He but join them on their troubled path, they will be sustained and cheered and filled with God-given strength to overcome the difficulties of their thorny way. They too may be witnesses of the power of the Great Physician to give health and joy to the broken heart.

Our poor faulty communications to each other in this time of our pilgrimage will soon be over. May we so speak that no word of ours, in gladness or in tears, may linger in a human heart to give secret pain or prompt to evil when our lips are closed in death, and we have gone to answer for thought, word, and deed in the sacred courts above!

## V.

## THE OLD TESTAMENT.

*Then opened He their understanding, that they might understand the Scriptures.* — LUKE xxiv. 45.

IT is the fashion in certain quarters to depreciate the Old Testament, to enhance by contrast the value of the New. This is much like taking away the foundation to increase the grandeur and security of the house.

Jesus Christ, as an historical character, must ever stand first among men. To the devout Christian He is far more, even the Lord from heaven. If we look to Him as authority and example, how definitely He fixes the estimate of the Old Testament. "It is written," was for our Lord an imperative sanction as to all points of doctrine and practice, and even His strong resource in the sorest assault of the tempter. In those last days of His intercourse with His disciples on earth, when He came to them in the majesty of One risen from the dead, it seems to have been His chief mission, when they were once convinced of His identity, to expound to them the Scriptures treating of Him and His great mediatorial work. Our Lord understood the meaning and value of revelation as no one else has ever understood them.

They who truly love the Lord Jesus will not be robbed of the beautiful Old Testament descriptions of the coming Messiah. How the inspired psalmist and the fervent prophets stamp on the mind the image of Him "by whose stripes we are healed," and who was "wounded for our transgressions, and bruised for our iniquity!" We cannot spare those types and foreshadowings that open the deep mysteries of redemption, and give us the Man of Sorrows to lean on in our utmost need. We cannot have blotted out the record of the Lamb of the continual sacrifice, forever pointing to the "Lamb of God who taketh away the sins of the world," the "Lamb slain from the foundation of the world," the Lamb to whom are lifted up heaven's songs of praise, the Lamb who, with the Father, is the light and the temple of the New Jerusalem!

We cannot give up the endeared and sacred names by which our Elder Brother is so impressively described by inspired historian and prophet and poet and judge. We cannot give up the story of those wonders wrought for the chosen people of God! We cannot give up the triumphs of faith by which "holy men of old" passed through danger and temptation and death. When we stand at some perilous point in life, with the strong enemies of past spiritual conflicts behind us, and before us the wild waves of the threatening future, how we welcome the remembrance of the deliverance of the children of Israel when they stood with the Red Sea before them, and the hosts of Pharaoh in their rear; and yet the command of the Lord was, "Go forward!"

The threatening waters were obedient to the God-given rod of Moses! We turn trustfully to the Leader stronger than the great lawgiver, sure that the "Captain of our salvation" will guide us safely all the way He has bidden us take to the Promised Land.

When tempted and overcome and smitten with the bite of the most venomous of all serpents, the poison-fangs of sin, we remember the writhing Israelites brought back from the gates of death by one look at the symbol raised aloft as a perpetual sign of the Great Healer. We lift our eyes to the cross of Calvary, we look, we repent, we believe, we are forgiven, and are at peace.

We cannot give up those dear old friends of our childhood whom we learned to know and

love as we gathered around our mother's knee,—
Joseph and Daniel and Ruth and Esther and Job;
and the Bible children too,— Naaman's little
maid, the lame Mephibosheth, and Samuel nurtured in the temple, and ever faithul to Israel's
God! We cannot give up the human old patriarchs, who are described as they were, with the
sins of their time upon them, but who, falteringly
taking the hand of the great God, were accepted
and forgiven. We have the promise of meeting
them in heaven, where all the redeemed shall
"sit down in the Kingdom."

We cannot give up those blessed Psalms which
through centuries on centuries have expressed
the aspirations, the repentance, the rapturous
exaltation, of the long line of saints who have
passed by grace to glory!

We cannot lose the Old Testament, with its
strong corroboration of the New! It is rooted
in our hearts; it has supported us in time past.

We yield to no man this strong staff of our
pilgrimage journey!

We will not give up, we must not give up, we
need not give up, we dare not give up, the precious treasure of the inspired Word of the Old
Testament!

What is the command of the Lord Jesus?
"Search the Scriptures!" Let us indeed search
them, "as one who seeketh for hid treasure."

May our eyes be more and more opened to their holy teaching, to the strengthening of our faith, and the enlightening of our minds to the true character of the Lord, just and righteous and full of compassion, whose day Abraham "saw and was glad."

## VI.

## THE SHEEP.

*Feed my lambs. Feed my sheep.* — JOHN xxi. 15, 16.

MUCH is said and written of the proper qualifications and preparation for the ministry. Much, doubtless, needs to be emphatically said as to gifts, learning, and inner life. The champion for Christ must be armed at all points, for warfare offensive and defensive. He must meet wickedness in high places and in the dark dens of vice, lukewarmness within the Church, and unbelief triumphant without. While all this is true, we must not forget that most important for the consecrated servant of Christ is the answer he can honestly give to the simple question, thrice urged by our Saviour on Peter before that disciple received his parting commission from the Great Shepherd of the Sheep.

How many students of theology, how many settled clergymen, how many exhorters and evangelists, how many mothers and Sunday-school teachers, if in their still solitude they should hear the voice of the Lord asking them, "Lovest thou Me?" would be shamed into an abashed and conscience-stricken silence! How few would dare to answer, "Thou, who knowest all things," Thou, who knowest my sins and my backslidings, "Thou knowest that I love Thee." Yet only they who can so answer have the essential element of the true call to the cure of souls.

In this personal love of Christ we have the secret of the success of many simple and unlearned men in so telling the "old, old story" that hearts are stirred and souls renewed.

Happily the true Christian life is ever developing, going on towards perfection. It may be quickened into existence where all before has been deadness and desolation. There are instances on record where clergymen who have begun their ministry in a cold and formal spirit have been awakened, through outer or inner experiences, to a sense of their individual needs and of the solemn responsibilities of a faithful shepherd of the sheep.

And what is it to feed the sheep? Of the domestic animals, the sheep perhaps needs the greatest care. Lavish nature spreads for him a banquet in the "green pastures and beside the still waters." Thither he is to be gently and persistently led. He must be watched, that he does not stray into dangerous places. He must be guarded from the ravenous beasts that would gladly devour him. A shelter must be provided for him, for night and cold and storm.

The sheep has his relish for food as a gift from God. That we cannot impart to him. We try to lead a friend, an ignorant sinner, an unbeliever, a circle of little children, to a true knowledge of the Lord Jesus. We find it impossible to give a single soul a desire, a relish for spiritual things. Let that be once sent by Heaven, then we feel that we can really feed the sheep, now longing for food. Let them who would feed the sheep of the Good Shepherd be instant and faithful in prayer that God will give this appetite for holy things to the souls to whom they would minister.

We may not, however, be satisfied with simply praying. We have here our responsibility for active exertion. Of the Heavenly Shepherd it is said, "He maketh me to lie down in green pastures, He leadeth me beside the still waters." This leading of the sheep to the food convenient for him, through the services of the sanctuary, the solemn sacraments, and the preached word, is the work of all the churches. Form and method there must be in this, as in all efforts that are lasting and effective; but not a stiff form, not an iron method.

The sheep are not tethered, each by himself, to graze upon his allotted bit of ground. The shepherd leads the flock in the open meadow or on the wild hillside, glad to see them, perhaps in groups here and there, feasting on a rich bit of pasture, or tasting the spring at the fountain-head. But there must be no wandering for tempting tufts on the edge of the hanging precipice, or venturing to dark thickets, the hiding-places of devouring beasts.

Sorrow and sickness and the bed of death are to human beings what night and storm and cold are to the humble sheep. For these times of peril, special provision must be made. They come to each soul separately, and the true pastor will care individually at such times for the members of his flock. Then he must gently urge the suffering sheep to the protection of the needed shelter. He must prayerfully lay the weary sheep in the arms of the only One who can bear him safely home. The solemn direct personal appeals that might have been rejected before, or have proved ineffectual, may not only now be welcomed, but abundantly blessed.

And as to the lambs, how are they to be fed? God gives the mother food for them to suffice for their tender infancy. So is it with the spiritual life of the child. Many a babe drawn to its mother's breast for its necessary food has at the same time all unconsciously received a blessing, sent from Heaven, through a mother's fond look of love and a mother's fervent prayer. She is, later, the first to clasp his baby hands, as a silent expression of assent to the petitions he cannot yet understand. So she leads him, little by little, to the "green pastures and the still waters." She has no stiff, conventional way with him. He follows naturally where she goes, happy at her side. He knows the spot where she daily bows the knee, and bows himself beside her, before he can realize the meaning of the attitude. He has found out the Book that is dearest to her, and the songs she best loves to sing. He learns to lisp the name that is for her "the name above all others." He loves the Lord Jesus first because she loves Him, and later he thanks Him for such a mother. So by degrees the child learns to share the spiritual food that is so welcome and strengthening to the mother.

With wise parents there will be no stuffing children with religious nourishment, no expectation of a development beyond their years. Yet children, too, must be methodically led in the spiritual life. Here a short time of family worship in the morning is most efficient. For their own sake, for the children's sake, parents should find time to lead their household in family prayer. They may have a fixed allegiance to their Heavenly King, but it is not so with the children. They have no confirmed, habitual longing for holy things. They live in the present. All things are new to them every morning. The joys and sorrows and even the teachings of yesterday are often with them altogether things of the past. They have no abiding sense of duty or responsibility. They have no stable affection for an ever-remembered Heavenly Father. With the new morning comes the fresh, eager interest in play and school and simple work and childish plans and undertakings. Their thoughts do not, like the lark, fly upward with the opening day. It has on them an immense influence to know that the whole household pays its united tribute of prayer and praise, gladly, lovingly, day by day, to the Great God above, whom the little ones, too, must learn to love and serve. A few such moments of family prayer, begun with a cheerful hymn in which the children soon willingly join, sends them on their way, rightly started for the coming day.

Nor must the children's own private prayers, morning and evening, be neglected. They must as soon as possible cease to be merely repeated prayers, but rather a natural expression of thankfulness, with added simple petitions for help and protection such as a child can really mean. So they must be led on to a true and affectionate intercourse with the Great and Loving Friend.

And the lambs on Sunday? How are they then to be fed? Freely, happily, abundantly. The Lord's Day is to be made to them a delight, not a bondage. But it is to be the Lord's Day, not to be given up, wholly or in part, to week-day interests or the pursuit of selfish pleasure. There should be a specially joyous, loving spirit in the family on Sunday.

More free time given by the father to the children on the First Day of the week, gives it a certain glad pre-eminence, and helps them by degrees to think of the Heavenly Father as One to be loved as well as revered.

The mother who has a full nursery, naturally wishing her servants all possible Sabbath rest and Sabbath privileges, has often but little time on Sunday to spare for her older children. On the father the duty so presses of keeping them happy and good; and it is a blessed duty. In its performance, little hands may draw him from the path of worldliness, and little lips prompt him to the trust and simplicity of which the child is the best teacher. The mother may have time for a hymn or two, sung with the eager group about her, or for a little pleasant, profitable reading aloud, but possibly no more. Happy for her if she herself can be so refreshed in the midst of her Sunday afternoon cares.

To the house of God the lambs in a truly Christian family soon learn to love to go. They are to be led thither, not driven. Where the parents go with evident joy, the children will soon wish to follow. A row of devout little children keeping up with the service as they best can, and happy to be at church, may perhaps unconsciously prove the most profitable sermon for some indifferent worshipper who has come to up to the courts of the Lord because it is seemly to do so.

The lambs must be guarded from bad companions, worse for them than the wild beasts for the helpless sheep. The wolf devours the lamb at once; but the bad companion poisons the life of the child and leaves him to a low existence, to his own misery and the contamination of his fellows.

Keep your little one, if you can, from bad companions, but he is not safest when most strictly penned in. When he does break loose, he will probably run as far as possible from the place of his confinement. Try to form his tastes and his principles, and by all means strive to keep his confidence. Let him know the kind of company you yourself enjoy, and would like to have for him. Have his schoolmates and friends about him sometimes under your own eye. Watch them and him as a guardian angel, not as a snappish house-dog, to have subject for growling.

Let love season all you do for your little ones. Above all, pray for and with your children. Christ loves the lambs. "It is not the will of your Heavenly Father that one of these little ones should perish." Prayer, purity, and patience will in the end have their perfect work.

Remember that in feeding the lambs you are yourself drawing near to the Good Shepherd. What you do for them you do for Him. In the end, when our Elder Brother gathers His own, may you be able to say joyfully, not one lacking, "Here am I, with the children God has given me!"

## VII.

### DAILY BREAD.

*Children, have ye any meat?* — JOHN xxi. 5.

HUMAN nature runs to extremes. Once heartily determined to cast off the bonds of the world, the flesh, and the devil, it imagines for itself a purely spiritual religion, above and beyond all earthly cares and interests, rather than a new life thrown into all old activities and relations and affections. The Christian man longs to be a pure spirit. God has linked him with a body and set him among his fellows to be loving and honest and pure and true.

The whole tenor of the Saviour's example and teaching is calculated to counteract all tendency to the overstrained and unnatural. Let once the divine life have been implanted in the soul, our Lord will have it developed like the quickening seed, to adorn and bless the place where it is appointed to grow. He was not pitched too high for human sympathies. Preaching and healing, supplying physical needs and soothing and uplifting sorrowing hearts, went hand in hand with Him. He whose mandate could call back the ruler's little daughter from beyond the gates of death could yet, in homely phrase, remind the rejoicing parents to give the rescued child "something to eat."

After our Lord's resurrection He appeared miraculously among His disciples and discoursed to them of the sublime mysteries of the Kingdom; yet He could sit down simply with the two friends at Emmaus, or tenderly ask the weary, disappointed fishermen by Tiberias, "Children, have ye any meat?" and satisfy, too, their pressing needs.

Let us treasure up this question of our Lord's for our comfort in this work-a-day world. It encourages us to dare to go to Him for help in all the affairs and interests that encompass us in our outward life. He will give us our daily bread as well as forgive us our trespasses, and keep us from temptation and lead us into the Heavenly Kingdom.

With regard to our spiritual life, too, our Lord comes to us with the striking words, "Children, have ye any meat?" Sometimes, in answer to His tender questioning, the Christian soul would tell its Lord of its unsatisfied wants. It would say, "I have no pastor, no devout friend to whom

I can open my doubts and struggles and perplexities. He who should teach me in the house of God is too dull in his own spiritual life, or too little gifted, to give me, Sunday after Sunday, the help I so bitterly need. I go to the sanctuary hungering and thirsting, and come empty away." This would be the statement of many an inexperienced Christian longing to be counselled and led in the way of life.

There are times with almost every true follower of our Lord when the depths of sorrow or anxiety or spiritual distress are to be passed through alone, as far as human comforters are concerned. May not this be the discipline sent of God to lead the harassed and afflicted one to close and trustful communion with the Heavenly Friend?

When we think the appointed messenger gives us no satisfactory food in the sanctuary, the Lord is still there, "where two or three are gathered together in His name." He has ever a sure blessing for all who are "truly seeking His face." Let the souls that are "hungering and thirsting in a dry and parched land" make at least for themselves the house of God a house of prayer, and their souls will be fed abundantly, and satisfied with water from the living spring.

The practical question, "Children, have ye any meat?" should be on the lips and in the hearts of the followers of the merciful Lord, as addressed to the suffering poor. In our homes of comfort we too often forget the very existence of the hungry and the houseless. When we do not see the poor, it may be for us as if they did not exist. If once, while we sat at our abundant meal, we could suddenly see, in a vision, our glad family table circled about by starving children, whose faces, haggard with want, and old before their time, looked with ravenous eagerness at our inviting fare, how the heart would be moved! We could not touch a morsel before we had fed the hungry we had too long forgotten in our land of plenty.

Think of these little ones, if you will, sometimes when you take your daily food, or sit down at your feasts, and you must for them freely open heart and purse. At that moment of real feeling, let wisdom come to your aid to show how and where and when such children should not only be temporarily fed, but be taught by honest labor to earn their daily bread.

And those boys and girls who lack "the meat that perisheth," have they sustaining nourishment for their tempted souls? Look at the little ones near to you by the ties of blood. How you shrink from the thought of their being even contaminated by the knowledge of the sin in the midst of which these outcast children must live.

How anxious you are to have your dear children take early the Saviour's offered hand, and be led in the ways of purity and joy. Have you no love to spare for the children who in the homes of want are breathing the very atmosphere of vice? They, too, have souls to be washed and made white in the blood of the Lamb. The Good Shepherd is their Shepherd too. He hears their far-away bleating in the wilderness of sin. He bids you see to it that they are brought home to the fold, to rejoice with your own little ones one day in heaven.

## Ascended.

I. Lost and Found.
II. A Miracle.
III. Union.
IV. Dying Eyes.
V. A Voice from Heaven.
VI. Persecution.
VII. Penitents.
VIII. Gentiles.
IX. Cheer.
X. Weakness.
XI. Priests.
XII. Churches.

# Ascended.

## I.

### LOST AND FOUND.

*He lifted up His hands, and blessed them. . . . While He blessed them, He was parted from them, and carried up into heaven.* — LUKE xxiv. 50, 51.

POETS and painters, and even preachers, impressed with the beauty and glory of the ascension of our Lord, seem to have striven to keep in our minds the idea of our Master gone from us, lost in a cloud, shut out from us, until He shall appear again in majesty to judge both the quick and the dead.

The human life of our Saviour finished, indeed, when He was received up again to the bosom of His Father. Yet why should we, like the awed disciples, still stand gazing up into heaven? Our Lord was from the time of His ascension to be no longer approached only in the one place where He could appear in His mortal form. He was to be henceforward present in all homes, and indwelling in all hearts that would receive Him. He was not to be the companion and friend alone of the little company of faithful ones whom He had gathered around Him during His short ministry, but of all those who through them should believe in His name. The King, the Messiah of the Jews, had become the Redeemer of all the nations of the earth.

This is our inheritance. Let us not stand gazing up into the impenetrable heavens, lost in trying to imagine the glories not yet revealed to us. Let us rather fold our hands in humility, and pray, with the blind man, to see Jesus walking at our side. We need to feel the presence of our Lord, drawing near to us with human sympathies, but with the divine riches of inexhaustible love, infinite patience, illimitable willingness to help, and almighty power to fashion our souls, comfort us in our sorrows, and deliver us in our dangers.

This is the Saviour we need. This is the Saviour who is given to us, through His finished work. We are no longer strangers and outcasts, we are no longer aliens and slaves. We may, through the Great Substitute, our Elder Brother, be forgiven children of the Heavenly Father and "fellow-citizens of the house of God." Born into the kingdom, bought with the blood of the Lamb, we may journey joyfully to the Heavenly Home.

Holding his nail-pierced hands out to bless, our Lord passed at His ascension from human eyes. It was His last expression of full forgiveness of His enemies, and His love for the world He had redeemed.

Do we so deal with those who have wounded and despised us? Have we "the mind of Christ"? Come we with blessings to those who have wronged us? Can we further their happiness, and delight to minister to their needs? This is the spirit of those who would "ascend up where Christ has gone before." There have been Christians who, in a wild transport of expectation of the near coming of Christ in glory, have left their ordinary occupations, in the hopes of so fixing their eyes on heaven as to be doubly ready to greet the Lord at His great Second Advent. Such enthusiasts have even prepared for themselves special white robes, in which, free from all stains of earth, they hoped to mount in the air and join the Lord with His glorious train of saints and angels.

Alas for poor mortality! We cannot form for ourselves a purity that shall make us fit for the Kingdom of Heaven. It is only the Master of the marriage feast who can give us the wedding garment. We must wait to be "clothed upon," when "mortality shall be swallowed up in life." We do not wing our way to the skies. In the midst of ordinary, every-day occupations we must mount upward, step by step, through faithfulness, humility, and self-sacrifice. We climb the "Hill Difficulty" leaning on our Lord, but while in the body we walk an earthly road. Here we are to serve, not reign. Here we are to pray, not prophesy. Here we are to follow, not lead. Here we are to live in meekness, not majesty. Here we are to strive to be like our Elder Brother, when "found in fashion as a man." *There* we shall be with Him and see Him as He is. There, in the kingdom of the Father, He will not be ashamed to call us brethren.

Faithfully walking our humble path here below, we shall welcome the summons of our Heavenly Master, whether it be "to meet the Lord in the air," or to sleep in Jesus, to wake in glory.

## II.

## A MIRACLE.

*When the Comforter is come, whom I will send unto you from the Father, even the Spirit of Truth, which proceedeth from the Father, He shall testify of Me.* — JOHN xv. 26.

IT is a common saying that the days of miracles are over. Yet there is a supernatural wonder in our days, which gives perpetual witness to the mighty power of God. When a man is suddenly changed in his aims, his hopes, his tastes, and his affections, a great wonder has been wrought. When the openly vicious begin to strive for the sake of Jesus, and, relying on His help, to lead a sober, pure, and useful life, and even succeed in the undertaking, they give strong testimony to the power of the Spirit of God. The opening of the eyes of the man born blind seems hardly more the result of a superhuman power than the change that makes the late worldling, or profligate, or criminal, a man walking in the ways of simplicity, virtue, and holiness.

These great changes are all marked by one distinguishing trait. The power of the Holy Ghost in the heart of man shows itself by opening the spiritual eyes to the character, work, commands, and promises of Jesus of Nazareth. Sometimes the converted soul, but late sunk in sin, seems almost transported by a view of the purity, the holiness, the indescribable love of Christ, and His amazing sacrifice for sin.

Who has not seen instances where from this ecstastic beginning had been developed the rounded, beautiful life of the mature Christian?

But to begin well is not always to end well. This period of rapturous acceptance of the great truths of religion has been known to pass away without producing the corresponding change in the outer and inner life. This joyous clearness in seeing for a time the beauty and preciousness of the Redeemer's life and teaching, remarkable as it is, is not enough to produce the great miracle of which we are speaking. It is, when it stops here, a half work, an uncompleted thing.

The commands of our Lord Jesus should be as dear to the Christian as His promises, and as affectionately responded to for His sake. That is a safe form of rapturous devotion to the great Elder Brother which gratefully welcomes every opportunity to do in His name the unwelcome duty, or forego the favorite sin. That is a sure work of the Holy Ghost which opens the eyes to the deceitfulness of the human heart, as well as to the "glory of the King in His beauty." That is a true conversion which prompts to penitence and purity as well as to psalms of praise.

For the golden fields of the harvest we must have the God-given seed, the heaven-sent rain and sunshine; but we must have also the timely work of the sower, the patient toil of the husbandman, and the glad garnering of the faithful reaper. So is it in the kingdom of grace. God gives freely and abundantly, but on His own conditions.

There are persons who perhaps honestly pray for the work of the Holy Spirit in their hearts, and then go their way to their pleasures and their cares, their absorbing pursuits or their morbidly nurtured sorrows, as if they themselves had nothing further to do with the matter.

The Spirit will take of the things of Christ and show them to us, but we must look to be healed. We must day by day take time to dwell on the life and character, the words and the works, of our Lord, and try to become so impressed by their preciousness and importance to us that in our leisure moments our thoughts turn as naturally to such meditations as do the child's to his play, or the mother's to her little ones.

The closet and the sanctuary, the Word and

the sacraments, the book of nature and the voice of friendly counsel, honest labor and well-earned rest, prosperity and adversity, joy and sorrow, family affection and social intercourse, the wise book or the lone meditation, the poor and the penitent, the sunshine and the shadows of life, may be so blessed to the seeker of sanctification as to become to him channels of divine grace.

He who folds his hands and sits statue-like to be made a saint, may be a cold image of a Christian, but never a living likeness of the living Lord. We must seek God if we would find Him; and He is ever found of them who truly seek Him.

The disciples waited at Jerusalem in prayer and supplication after the glorious parting at Olivet. When, on the day of Pentecost, they were filled with a strange power, above and beyond their own personality, how joyous must have been their conviction that the Lord, who is the Truth as well as the Life, had remembered His promise, and sent to them the Comforter to bide with them always! What an encouragement they now had to ask all things in His name, who could so redeem His pledge! Now they were freshly linked to the Friend who seemed to have passed from them to a far, foreign land. He had sent them a token of His continual remembrance of their needs. They were in touch with Him once more. Not once alone was this blessing given. It was henceforward to be a means of perpetual intercourse with the Lord of their future home, and a wonderful power to prepare them for its endless joys.

What that glorious gift was to the first disciples it may be to us. It is for us the same encouragement to prayer that it was to them,— even that the faithful Lord is ever true to His word. We may not expect to work their miracles, or to speak with tongues as they did, but there are wonders to be worked in us in the sanctification of heart and life. Who is it among us who is really trying to order thought, word, and deed after the perfect law, who does not find here a work too great for human power? Here the divine aid must be granted, or we cannot come off conquerors. The "unruly member" must be robbed of its deadly poison, and taught to speak the loving language of "the kingdom." The heart-springs must be cleansed by the living water. These great miracles are the work of the Holy Spirit, for which we must persistently pray. We must pray for the spirit of sanctification; but while we pray we must watch and work. Living the life of love, prayer, and watchfulness, we shall persevere unto the end.

## III.

## UNION.

*That they may be one; as Thou, Father, art in Me, and I in Thee, that they may be one in us.* — JOHN xvii. 21.

OUR Elder Brother, in His teaching, now lifted up the poor things of earth to be the symbols of things heavenly, and now solemn mysteries from above were allowed to be examples for our humble imitation in our simple, every-day life. The household objects about us in our homes were thus taught a speech by which to remind us of holy counsel and a heavenly dwelling-place. Great truths, too deep for our full comprehension, were made to be to us in our earthly walk a source of guidance and consolation.

There is, there must be, much in the Bible that exceeds our poor comprehension; but our Saviour has illustrated and simplified much that it is difficult for us to grasp. We might not have dared to compare the divine unity with our poor fellowships here below. Our Lord, who so well knew the oneness of the God of Love, has set it before us as an example. He prayed for all who should believe in His name "that they may be one as we are one."

God has given us the family as a perpetual embodiment of the truth that love is the one principle of real unity in the midst of diversity. It has been said that for the exercise of the highest affection there should be love between two, and a mutually shared affection for a third object or some great outside interest. This is specially exemplified by the structure of the family. The husband and wife, dear to each other, have a common devotion to their little ones. Brothers and sisters have their reciprocal affection and their filial love. Yet how often the seeds of discord spring into rank, unwholesome growth in the very bosom of the family. Where there should be oneness there may be envy and jealousy, contention and alienation.

Selfishness may prompt husband or wife to be dissatisfied with the way influence or rule is shared between the heads of the family. The shy husband may even feel himself cast into the shadow by the brilliant conversational powers of the wife. Even a loving wife may sometimes find herself almost crushed by the force and wisdom and attainments of the husband. She may be depressed and extinguished in the presence of him whom she so cordially admires.

Self dies hard in human nature. The once strong-minded father may think it trying to see in his declining years that it is his brilliant son who now draws around him the eager, listening circle, while the remarks of the old man are hardly heard at all, or little regarded. The mother may be wounded as she sees time after time the love of her early friends grow cold towards her, while it has taken new life towards her winning daughter.

Envy, jealousy, and selfishness cause these painful feelings, which are not the less sinful and destructive of inner peace because they are hidden from human eyes, in the depths of the turbulent heart.

Among brothers and sisters the struggle for pre-eminence, or the contests about mine and thine, may creep in, even to make the nursery a scene of quarrels,— the promise of the lifelong bickerings and small rivalries that take the place of true brotherly affection.

Mutual love makes a family a blessed unity. Without love a family is only an aggregate of uncongenial items.

Our Lord prays for His followers, "That they may be one, as Thou, Father, art in Me, and I in Thee, that they also may be one in us, that the world may know that Thou hast sent Me." To reach this loving unity must be the aim of the Church Catholic!

When one throb of love for our Elder Brother and for all His true followers passes round the world as the electric current speeds from land to land, then will all the nations begin to be indeed of the kindgom of our Lord and His Christ.

We can each do something to bring about that happy day, by suppressing in ourselves party prejudice, and using our influence against the animosity of a contentious spirit of division. We can join hand in hand with all them who love the Lord Jesus in sincerity and truth, and give them a brotherly greeting. We can own the likeness of the Master wherever we see it. We can acknowledge a fellow-disciple who does not use the same attitude in prayer that we do, or sing the same sacred songs, or have the name of the same country or the same man as the label of the Church to which he belongs.

Let us "love as brethren, be pitiful, be courteous;" and true Christian sympathy will increase by exercise, and win responsive warmth. So shall we grow in likeness to the God of Love, Father, Son, and Holy Ghost.

## IV.

## DYING EYES.

*Behold, I see the heavens opened, and the Son of Man standing at the right hand of God.* — ACTS vii. 56.

WHEN our friends pass away to the Better Country, we have heard their last words, we have seen their dear faces for the last time on earth. Not so was it with the departure of our Elder Brother from the scene of His great work here below.

As we know something of our Lord's life and His high and solemn purpose before He was the Babe of Bethlehem, so we are also permitted to have tidings from Him after He was received up into heaven. We have the evidence as well as the assurance that He is "the same yesterday, to-day, and forever."

To see Jesus in His glory was, as far as we know, first granted to faithful Stephen, in the midst of his martyrdom. "He, being full of the Holy Ghost, looked up into heaven and saw the glory of God, and Jesus standing at the right hand of God." What wonder that after such a revelation he was so lifted above mortal pain and fear that in the midst of the fast-falling stones he "fell asleep"!

Stephen really saw his Master and spoke to Him when he said, "Lord Jesus, receive my spirit.... Lord, lay not this sin to their charge!" Faith had been changed to sight while he was yet in the body. Who can tell how many of the persecutors of Stephen went home believers in the Jesus to whom the martyr had so evidently spoken, and who had given him power to pass peacefully through a cruel death!

Since the time of Stephen, many true Christians seem to have had their eyes opened to see in the dying hour something of the glory awaiting them beyond the dark river. Who has not had, among his circle of friends, devout believers who have been permitted to see in their last moments Him who had long been their dearest companion? Others have murmured of visions of angels, others of the well-beloved face of a sainted mother or a departed friend, welcoming them to the Heavenly Home. Dying eyes have been filled with rapture, the lips could not speak, and the still, cold face was stamped with the impress left by the joy and peace of a glad foretaste of heaven in the moment of departure. This is sight, not merely faith.

That no such revelation has been granted to this or that dying Christian must not be taken as an evidence against the reality of his spiritual life. God deals out His special blessings in the kingdom of grace, as in the providential world, as seemeth to Him best. He has His great purposes for us and the souls about us, in the way in which He leads us even to the gates of heaven.

To one He gives the angels' sight in the dying hour. Another, beyond the dark tomb, may have the tender welcome, "Blessed are they who have not seen, and yet have believed!" How many faint-hearted Christians, discouraged and despairing under mere ordinary worries and disappointments, pant for the martyr's sight, while all unprepared to show the martyr's courage in the time of trial. They want to grasp the crown, but will not bear the cross!

Work, not rapture, is the usual portion of the believer's commonplace path. Patient continuance in well-doing, with persistent penitence and prayer, bring quiet joy and peace. Love to our fellow-men lifts us slowly up to God. They who have humbly looked down to find some lowly work for Christ will surely one day look up to heaven to see Him, "not through a glass, darkly, but face to face."

## V.

## A VOICE FROM HEAVEN.

*Much more shall not we escape, if we turn away from Him that speaketh from heaven.* — HEB. xii. 25.

APOSTLES in the midst of the trials of their ministry were privileged to hear again and again the voice they best loved, and to have words of cheer from the ascended Lord. He spoke not only for them, but for us also. The express command concerning the revelation made to the honored John at Patmos was, "What thou seest, write in a book." Of those who should receive this precious testimony it is plainly said, "Blessed is he that readeth!" It is even written, "It is I, Jesus, who have sent mine angel to testify these things to you in the churches."

How worthy of our affectionate, careful study are all the known words spoken from heaven by our ascended, glorified Elder Brother! How solemn for us is the warning, "Much more shall not we escape, if we turn away from Him that speaketh from heaven!"

And how tender and loving are many of these our Lord's utterances from the throne to His struggling foster-brethren below!

"Behold, I stand at the door and knock." Our Royal Brother is with us in heart, yet "without," beyond the sorrows and sufferings of this lower world, outside of our sphere of vision, too often far from our thoughts, hidden from our souls in our utter absorption in the cares and follies of this visible world. Our Lord, our Master, is knocking at our lowly door. He comes from His throne of glory to our poor hearts, and bids us let Him in. He comes out as our Judge and King. In the simple, familiar words of earthly friendship, He pleads to come in and sup with us. He will lay aside His royal dignity, and be to us as our nearest and dearest on earth, with whom we share our daily food, and the sweet intercourse of family life. So our Lord speaks to us, His poor unworthy brethren.

And how is it with us? We would have Him far away in His glory, to be prayed to at stated times, to be worshipped in the hallowed sanctuary, to be met occasionally at His Holy Table, after a solemn time of repentance and sacred preparation.

Not so alone our Master would meet with us. He would come to us in our ordinary daily life, to sanctify all we do or think or say,— to make holy our simplest joys and interests. He would be with us at table, "about our bed," walk with us by the way, join us with our guests, take us by the hand on the couch of sickness and in the dying hour.

Shall we let Him knock in vain? Shall we close to His tender appeal the hearts we have given to Him? Shall we answer to His friendly knock, "Not now, Lord! In heaven we shall be ever with Thee. Here we must lead our work-a-day life, apart from Thy holy presence"?

Nay! Let the Lord purify our walk and conversation. Let them be what He hath cleansed, and so "not common or unclean."

Let us open our hearts and our homes, that our Lord may be always with us, that He may dwell with us, going no more out, and consecrating all we do and are, until we go in with Him to His Upper Kingdom!

For our guidance on the way let us cherish every word of our Saviour, whether spoken in His mysterious union with the Father, before He was the Son of Mary, or during His earthly ministry, or when in the "voice like many waters," from His abundant glory, He warned and counselled and comforted with unfailing tenderness the faltering, wandering children of men!

## VI.

## PERSECUTION.

*I am Jesus, whom thou persecutest.* — ACTS ix. 5.

IT strikes us with wonder that our Lord could say, even when He was in human form, of all ministry to suffering man, "Inasmuch as ye have done it unto one of the least of these My brethren, ye have done it unto Me." It is even more difficult to grasp the great fact that in the midst of the joys at the right hand of God the ascended Lord could so feel Himself one with His humble followers that He could make to the affrighted Paul the declaration, "I am Jesus, whom thou persecutest."

What had the wrongs of those lowly men and women in that little spot of earth to do with the "Only Begotten Son, full of grace and truth," in the glory of His Father's presence?

Our Lord in His great compassion has chosen to link Himself, the Head with the body, even the Church of faithful believers. Ascended into heaven, it had not pleased Him to sever that connection. He could feel the sufferings of His humblest members, and count their persecution as directed against Himself. Our sense of our unworthiness to be brought into this sacred relation with our Great Redeemer fosters a kind of unbelief in this most consoling of realities. As the soul resides in the body and permeates and influences its every part, so, it is revealed to us, our Master dwells, after His wonderful fashion, in the hearts of His true servants one and all. "Know ye not that Christ dwelleth in you, except ye be reprobates?"—"I in them, and they in Me."

Let us welcome with deep adoration this great mystery, in which the Lord makes us, His poor human children, His temple, consecrated to His use. And let us not stupidly and self-righteously assume that we individually alone are to have this privilege, or that it is limited to the small body of Christians to which we ourselves belong. Let us respect the humblest and most faltering of the servants of Christ as a part of His body, — a trifling part, a diseased part possibly; yet a part to be healed and exalted and made useful through the indwelling power of God.

Let us not set ourselves on a pinnacle, as so perfect in the interpretation of the Word that we may cast out in scorn the self-denying followers of Christ who may differ from us in some minor point of doctrine, at best but dimly revealed, lest we hear the voice of the Master saying, "I am Jesus, whom thou persecutest in the form of My blinded and devoted disciple."

We are not to suppose that in the early days of the Church, when converts were suddenly made by thousands, they were all deeply versed in the subtle truths of the new religion. Indeed, we know through the inspired Epistles that many of those first Christians were in darkness as to what we might now consider cardinal points of belief and practice. Yet they had a devotedness that risked all for the cause of Christ. They would rather die than deny their Master, and He was so one with them that He reckoned their persecution as persecution of Himself.

If our Lord so unites Himself with the whole Church, how specially He must consider Himself represented by the appointed ambassadors who preach and minister in His name. An ambassador at an earthly court must be honored, because he represents his sovereign and his people. He may be awkward and uncouth, and personally unworthy, but he must receive a certain amount of outward respect, as he stands, not for himself, but for the power from which he is accredited. To his own master he is responsible for what he is, and for his fitness for the office he holds.

An indulged, unfounded dislike for this or that clergyman, for what he is privately and personally, a light criticism of his manners and peculiarities, an assumption of superiority in speaking of him, as if he were responsible to the critic for his amount of gifts and graces, may seem trifling offences; yet by disrespect to a clergyman, an undeserved reproach cast on his person and name, his influence may be slowly undermined, and his office brought into contempt. The Lord, identifying Himself with His servant and ambassador, may whisper reproachfully to the self-satisfied fault-finder and scandal-monger, "I am Jesus, whom thou persecutest."

It is a serious matter, that touches the honor of the King of kings. Let those who know *certainly* of real wrong-doings by such authorized messengers of the Gospel be ready to suffer themselves for the purifying of the Church. Let them be willing to testify openly against such offenders before the proper authorities, and so have them lawfully deposed. This is a far better way to show zeal for truth and righteousness than by casting slurs upon the whole clerical body, or privately denouncing this or that clergyman as unfit to minister at the altar.

What a solemn responsibility rests on the clergy, who so particularly and officially represent the Heavenly King! How pure they should be in life and conversation, how above all reproach! How sound they should be in doctrine! How diligent they should be in their high calling! How they should shine with the brightness of them who are much "on the Mount" in sweet, loving communion with the Great Head of the Church!

It is not alone private Christians and clergymen who are honored images and substitutes of the King of kings. We have His messengers in the nursery and the hovel, in the hospital, and even sometimes in the prison. If we withhold rights from the lowly, freedom to worship from the devout, and help from the needy, to us comes the voice of reproof, "I am Jesus, whom thou persecutest."

David could cherish the lame Mephibosheth, and welcome the unfortunate cripple to the royal table, for the sake of the princely friend of his humble youth. Is there no sufferer you can succor for the sake of a higher Prince, who has given you a share in His birthright, and an inheritance with Him in His kingdom?

Observing children might tell of flattering guests who have praised and caressed them in the presence of their parents, but, meeting them in other society, have shown a profound indifference to their merits and attractions. How do we meet the despised, the distressed of this world, when forgetful that the eye of the Great Friend of all is upon us?

Let us beware lest we, now heartlessly indifferent to the sufferings of our brethren, should hear, at the last solemn Day of Retribution, the voice of the Judge Himself pronouncing our doom in the words, "I am Jesus, whom thou hast persecuted!"

# VII.

## PENITENTS.

*I am with thee, and no man shall set on thee to hurt thee: for I have much people in this city.* — ACTS xviii. 10.

THE gold ring and the goodly apparel are always in the Father's house for the returning penitent. The Lord Jesus has His own special mercies for those who have wandered into a far country. In their deep sense of their own sinfulness they need an unusual assurance that their souls, too, can be "washed and made white in the blood of the Lamb."

To see the ascended Lord, to be spoken to by Him again and again, were Paul's seal, not only of the authority of his apostleship, but of his own free and full forgiveness. As such, he accepts them humbly and gratefully, never forgetting to think of himself as the "chief of sinners."

Paul, who knew the converting power of God in the experience of his own strong manhood, had hope for all to whom he could preach the Gospel. To Festus and Agrippa, to jailers and prisoners, to idolaters and pharisees, he could tell the story of the cross, believing it possible that the miracle that had been wrought in him could be repeated in the souls of his hearers. He was a living witness of the truth and power of the Gospel which he preached.

To speak fearlessly to the Jews and Gentiles in idolatrous Corinth he had a double encouragement. In a vision of the night, the voice of the Lord had said to him, "Be not afraid, but speak and hold not thy peace; for I am with thee, and no man shall set on thee to hurt thee, for I have much people in this city."

In the wonderful list which Paul has given of the afflictions and dangers and sufferings through which he had passed, we have a clear evidence that his Master did not mean that he should be spared pain or peril or difficulty in his work as an apostle. He was but to be strengthened by the thought that it was not in the power of infuriated man to injure one to whom the Lord had said, "I have chosen thee," "I am with thee."

Evil men may assail the Christian. They may defame or belie him, degrade him in the eyes of whole communities, but they cannot hurt him if his name is written in heaven. He is safe in the midst of the wildest storms, for Jesus is with him in the ship.

How little could Paul imagine that the Lord had much people in corrupt and heathen Corinth,— that the Good Shepherd was seeking those wandering sheep in that worse than wilderness.

Discouragements await the active Christian, wherever he may have his field of labor. He must be often tempted to withdraw his hand from his work, in helpless despair. Let such workers ever remember our Lord's loving expression of ownership in the future Christians of Corinth.

Perhaps we see only dead souls and obstinate offenders where the Lord sees His own people who are to come out from their sins and be "sons and daughters to the Lord Almighty."

There will be joy in heaven if you can win one wanderer from the error of his ways, or help one puzzled, stumbling pilgrim on the narrow upward path. You may work and pray, and believe that the Lord will bless all that you undertake in His cause. You may have an abundant harvest where all has seemed barrenness and blight.

Labor in the loving spirit of your Master, not as if you were on one side and the wrong-doers on the other, opposed and inimical. You are working for your brethren,— love and seek them as brethren. Look for the lost sheep with the mind of the Good Shepherd. Remember that it is only through the abounding grace from on high that you yourself have been brought home to "the Shepherd and Bishop of your soul."

# VIII.

## GENTILES.

*Depart, for I will send thee far hence unto the Gentiles.*
ACTS xxii. 21.

THE Jews are not the only nation who have looked upon all of a different race as fit for scoffing and reproach. It is not alone the Chinese who regard all other peoples as mere outside barbarians. We are all tainted with the same exclusiveness.

Extravagant claims to superiority, which a man would shrink from putting forward for himself individually, he does not hesitate loudly to vindicate for the nation of which he is a citizen.

In some quarters the unchristianized world is so thoroughly despised that the missionary to distant idolaters is looked upon as a mistaken fanatic or a drivelling weakling.

"Why not look after the heathen in our midst?" say these objectors, with no little show of truth. Yes! Why not look after the heathen in our midst? Let that be done thoroughly and faithfully. At the same time let not the command be neglected which bids us "teach all nations" the way of life.

It is a singular fact that the objectors to foreign missions are rarely themselves active in bearing the Gospel to the heathen at their doors. Most commonly they comfortably sit inactive in their own pleasant homes, perhaps within gunshot of the homes of poverty and sin. Some of the most devoted foreign missionaries have been first zealous workers among the poor and wicked at home. These devout men and women, moved with pity for "the nations that know not God," have left all to enlighten the dark places of the earth. May God bless these noble pioneers, and wake up the dwellers at ease to something of their zeal in the good cause at home or abroad!

For special work among the Gentiles our Lord was pleased to choose one of the most gifted, instructed, and devoted of His followers, and even to single him out for peculiar honor. Again and again the ascended Lord Himself spoke words of encouragement to Paul, and indicated and located his work. The persecuting Saul was to become the persecuted Paul, the great Apostle to the Gentiles. Let the Christian mother never despair of seeing her wayward sons the children of God. The might of divine grace is boundless. The power of prayer is immeasurable. Hedley Vicars, recklessly plunging into the wild career of a young soldier at a foreign station, was to have in the future the blessed work of leading as a Christian officer his fellows and his subordinates, not only in the front of battle, but to the better victory over the world, the flesh, and the devil.

A long line of mothers, before and after the untiring Monica, could point to their noble sons and say, "Behold the results of earnest, faithful prayer!" Such wandering sons, once turned towards the upward path, are sure to be eager workers for the good of their fellow-men. They may have neither the power of Paul nor of Apollos, but God will appoint them a field of labor, and bless their every honest effort to win others from what they know to be the way of danger and death.

There is one whole class of men who have a world-wide mission. They are at one time in so-called Christian ports; at another in the lone islands of the ocean; at another in the crowded cities of the East. The seamen on merchant vessels, in the whalers of the North, and in the ships of proud navies, where do they not go? What traces do they leave behind them in the lands they visit? What picture of Christian manhood do they paint for the peoples with whom they have intercourse?

This is the era in the Church when lay workers are brought to the front, to stand side by side with the clergyman in the great struggle. In ministering to the poor, in the cause of temperance, and even in preaching the Word in cottage and street and mine, and sometimes in the Sabbath assembly, the layman is actively at work. Nor is he idle on the sea. There are pious sailors who make their ships a Bethel, and who, free-handed, bear the printed Bible and the instructive book to the nations whose language they cannot speak. The faces of such hardy sailors, telling of body subject to spirit, and both gladly devoted to the Lord, must make an impression wherever they are seen. Alas that there are so few such workers among the men of the sea! Let the quiet dwellers on land do their part to increase this missionary band. Let them provide more Christian homes for Jack in their own great cities, in which he can be protected from temptation. Let such homes be ready for him in foreign ports, where, in the warm gush of gladness at being on shore again, he may have his heart taught to lift itself in thankfulness to the God who preserved him from the dangers of the sea, and to devote himself henceforward to the faithful service of the Captain of our Salvation. Let him there be reminded of his mother's teaching and his mother's prayers. Let good books be provided for the quiet moments of the sailor on board ship, books to keep him from unprofitable talk and amusements, and to give him a happy, instructive hour, and books, above all, to lead him in the way of life.

Let the seaman be properly ministered to by the landsman, and we shall have a band of self-supporting missionaries who will bear the Gospel to every shore, and show the unbeliever the living Christian man.

Many stay-at-home Christians have awakened to a sense of their duty towards the honest tars, but more must be done. Let us each and all have a part in truly Christianizing the men of the sea, who ever on their watery path are going "far hence to the Gentiles."

## IX.

### CHEER.

*Be of good cheer, Paul.* — ACTS xxiii. 11.
*He calleth his own sheep by name.* — JOHN x. 3.

HEDGED round by danger, how welcome it must have been to the great apostle to hear in the night the voice of his Master saying, "Be of good cheer, Paul!" To be called by name as brother speaks to brother!

In the midst of sorrows, discouragements, and temptations, let the child of God put his own familiar name in the place of Paul's, and listen to the Lord Jesus saying, "Be of good cheer, ——!" What trial would seem unendurable could you hear such a voice so speaking? Take hold gladly of the idea that you are not simply to the Lord as a stumbling follower, but as yourself, in all your individuality. By name you are known and loved by your Elder Brother in heaven.

"God is no respecter of persons." From our fellow-men we have titles of honor, or perhaps terms of contempt. From the palace to the poorhouse, from the crowned monarch to the crippled beggar, all are the same to the Lord, sinful human beings in need of a Saviour and Friend. He knows each of His wandering children by name.

How pleasant it is to the aged Christian who has seen his generation pass away, no one left to call him by the name of his boyhood, to remember that he is the same to the Lord Jesus as in his early days. His name is known in heaven, and the Lord is ever at his side to whisper, "Be of good cheer, —— !"

And what was the consolation given to Paul to encourage him to good cheer? His present danger was to pass by, but no flowery future was promised him. He was to have the privilege of witnessing for his Master at Rome, as he had witnessed for Him at Jerusalem. More life, more service, and more suffering were in store for him, therefore must he be of good cheer.

How often it happens that in the midst of active life, some faithful laborer is by the force of circumstances suddenly removed from his field of usefulness, and placed in a position where he is more like a caged creature than a free man. His natural powers seem deprived of their lawful action, his zeal but a burning pain within.

Let such a desponding soul hear the words,

"Be of good cheer,——! for as thou hast testified of Me in Jerusalem, so must thou bear witness also at Rome!" Patiently wait, and the time of usefulness will come again. God has no unnecessary tools in His workshop. They are all to be employed when and where it seemeth Him best.

"Be of good cheer!" is the motto for the whole Church, collectively as well as for each individual by name. Sin and unbelief may seem to prosper and threaten to triumph, but the great day must come when the Lord shall reign King of Nations, as He is King of Saints!

"Be of good cheer!" Pass it along the lines of the laborers in the great vineyard, weary with toil, and speaking drearily of the blighted harvest! Ring it out for the lone missionary in the far foreign land! Whisper it to the humble women ministering by sick-beds and in the homes of want! Say to them all, "Your labor is accepted, and in due time you shall reap an abundant blessing!"

And you, ye followers of the Light of the World, what brightness are you casting around your earthly path? Do you so rejoice in the Lord that you are sunshine in your home? Are you sour or bitter or murmuring for the ears for which you speak in your daily walk and conversation? Are you cast down by trifles and discouraged by slight obstacles? Have you no hope or consolation but success in the undertakings of the present hour? If this scheme or that enterprise should fail, would your all be lost? Have you no Heavenly Friend? Have you no hope beyond this fleeting life? If you are dejected, momentarily wrecked by every chafing disappointment, how are you different from a heathen in the same case? Have you no stay for small troubles as well as for great? Think you are spoken to by name, and to you the exhortation is, "Be of good cheer, ——!" Be cheerful in your daily life. Have the sunny face and the glad heart that befit the child of God journeying heavenward.

If the small cares and disappointments and mortifications of your common life so destroy your peace, can it be that your treasure is in heaven? On what is your heart fixed, and what is the source of your joy?

"Rejoice in the Lord, and again I say unto you, rejoice!" Wear a cheerful face, because you have a happy heart, unmoved by the passing cares and annoyances of earthly life. Be of good cheer, and you will be a source of cheer. Let your light so shine that you will lighten your household and home with the brightness reflected from the Sun of Righteousness!

# X.

## WEAKNESS.

*My strength is made perfect in weakness.* — 2 COR. xii. 9.

"MY strength is made perfect in weakness." Another of the precious utterances of the ascended Lord to the Apostle Paul, Paul's treasure first, and then a rich inheritance for all believers.

Weakness of body is generally considered a condition cutting off truly the possibility of lively pleasure, but happy in its freedom from positive pain. This is in many cases a true description. There can, however, be weakness to such an extent that soul and body seem to have lost the powers of organized life. There is no tension anywhere. All is relaxed. The mind is incapable of consecutive thought. The body shrinks from the slightest exertion. There is a weariness, an exhaustion, that is positively and painfully felt through the whole frame. An overwhelming sense of helplessness fills the eyes with tears, and drops the jaw in a powerlessness that is almost imbecility. The slightest interest in anything is so great an exertion that it beads the forehead with a cold perspiration that creeps like a chilly mist over the whole body and wraps the sufferer round, perhaps when he is alone in the dark night, with what seems like the very atmosphere of the cold, damp grave. Even at this climax there can come to the soul the comforting thought of the sympathy of the crucified Saviour. Human friends may talk lightly of this kind of suffering, or bid the patient be thankful it is not actual pain. The stricken invalid silently remembers Him whose sweat in the solemn garden was as great drops of blood, and who endured the long-drawn death of sacred Calvary. Our Lord feels for the weak as well as the tortured, and He can give a strength that is made perfect in weakness, a victory over nature that He best can understand.

The patient, loving smile of many a weak, wasted sufferer has been registered in heaven as a triumph as great as that which is courageously won on a bloody battle-field or in some strong man's struggle with a besetting sin.

There is, too, a spiritual weakness that is hard to bear, humiliating as it is, when the victim comes to a full consciousness of his condition. He sees himself overcome by the slightest temptation, now tossed by doubt, now harassed by a vacillating, unsteady purpose, — beginnings of good ending in a return to old habits of evil, — prayers begun in earnestness, but dispersed into wandering, unconnected thoughts of pleasure or care or sin. How many such a weak penitent has cried out in despair, "Wretched man that I am, who shall deliver me from the body of this death?" Here, also, the strength of the Lord may be made perfect in weakness. Let such a one remember the words of the great apostle, "When I am weak, then am I strong." Strong he was as the child is who lets himself be tenderly led by a wise and loving hand. He clasps that hand closely, takes one step at a time, without anxiously looking forward, fearing to fall. Conscious of weakness, the tottering, unstable Christian leans on Him who is mighty to save, leans trustfully, leans ever, goes forward, and is safe!

As it is with the weak Christian, so is it with the weak invalid. The sufferer from debility must cherish no fears for the future, must not think even of the endurance of the next hour. The present is sufficient. For the present, strength will be given. The hand may hang down feebly, the soul may seem unable to seek courage or help, but "underneath are the Everlasting Arms." He who is like the shepherd who "bears the lambs in his bosom and gently leads them that are with young" can carry you home, poor trembling one, unable even to lean on the Strong Stay. He who could speak so graciously to His ancient people, He who "bore and carried them all the days of old," will gently support you, as the eagle taketh her young on her wings and soars with them from mountain-top to mountain-top. "In quietness and confidence is your strength!" Your strength will be made perfect in weakness, and all the glory will be to Him who has loved us and has given Himself for us with an everlasting love.

## XI.

### PRIESTS.

*We have a Great High Priest.* — HEB. iv. 14.

AMONG the strongest ties that bind man to man is the bond that is knit between the soul and its spiritual father, that other soul that has led it to the cross, and is its guide towards heaven. Here there is always the danger of the blind devotion of the beginner in the Christian life, who looks up to his experienced friend or pastor as almost inspired, a saint upon earth, a necessary medium between him and God.

Even apostles must exclaim, "We are men of like passions as ye are!" in repelling the idolatrous worship thrust upon them.

A perfect priesthood is what all who would be themselves holy earnestly long for. God be praised, there are in all the churches men so sanctified that they are lifted as near heaven as is possible for poor human nature here below. We may love them and trust them and profit by their ministry, but we are not to set them on a pinnacle to be adored, or imagine that this or that man is necessary for our real growth in the spiritual life.

Strange to say, this devotedness to the hand that has led a man into the right path may degenerate into a selfish appropriation of the wise teacher. A lawful reverence and affection may be blended with the low spirit of contention between "mine" and "thine." "*My* pastor is the best," is the declaration too often heard in spirit, if not exactly so couched in words. All other preachers and Christian teachers must be depreciated, criticised, and, if possible, brought to contempt, to exalt the one man who has had the power to reach the soul of the speaker. Away with this kind of monopolizing of one noble instrument for good!

Devout clergymen suffer much from this blind devotion and foolish adulation. They want no flattering words after an earnest appeal, but the fruit in human souls of humble penitence and holy faith.

The priests of earth must have their own conflicts, but our High Priest, who stands ever in the presence of God for us, is without sin. He need offer no sacrifice for Himself. He is the pure offering, sufficient for the sins of the whole world.

We can imagine the solemn hush among the Jewish worshippers when once a year the high priest entered alone into the holy of holies, there to present the appointed sacrifice for his own sins and the sins of his people, in the presence of the Perfect and Almighty God. In helpless unworthiness the penitents stood without. So we stand here in our earthly lot. We are not yet admitted to the glory above, but there we have our Surety, our Representative, our Intercessor, our Elder Brother, who "appeareth in the presence of God for us." Our poor prayers are for His sake accepted. He is touched with a feeling for our infirmities, for He was tempted in all points like as we are, yet without sin. He offers again His loving prayer, the trustful wish of His divine yet human heart, "Father, I will that they also whom Thou hast given Me be with Me where I am." "Seeing, then, that we have a Great High Priest that is passed into the heavens, Jesus the Son of God, let us hold fast our profession. . . . Let us therefore come boldly unto the throne of grace, that we may obtain mercy, and find grace to help in time of need." Let us remember the blessed words, "He is able also to save them to the uttermost that come unto God by Him, seeing He ever liveth to make intercession for them."

Our High Priest shall come again to us from the great holy of holies. Then will he seal the full forgiveness He has even for us, with the glad words, "Come, ye blessed of my Father, inherit the kingdom prepared for you from the foundation of the world!"

# XII.

## CHURCHES AND CHURCH-MEMBERS.

*I, Jesus, have sent mine angel to testify unto you these things in the churches.* — REV. xxii. 16.

THERE are many who propose to reform churches. There are few who are in earnest about reforming themselves. If you find yourself in a church where you think devout, consistent Christians are few, make it your business soberly and solemnly to see to it that you are, in thought, word, and deed, living up to your own high standard of discipleship.

It may be that if you should go over to some other branch of the Church Catholic, or some other parish or congregation, you might find that what you most needed was not a change in church association, but the prayer of the converted Indian, "Lord, save me from that bad man, myself!"

Stay where you are if your objection to your church be the low state of piety among its members. If you think you have light, why not let it shine in what you consider a dark place? Go forward yourself in the Christian life! Take those around you by the hand,— your wife, your children, your servants, your employees, your friends,— and lead them, if you can, to a nobler, more Christ-like walk and conversation! You cannot, butterfly-like, flit hither and thither to enjoy your Christian course, your Christian feelings. You are to do the most good you can in your day and generation. Do you want to move your little candle into what you consider the full sunshine? Better that it should give light to your own house, the "household of faith," where the Providence of God has placed you.

A wise man has said, "The difficulties in this world are not so much the faults of organizations for high purposes, as in being able to find noble, holy men to make up such organizations, and wisely, fearlessly, and conscientiously to work in them and through them." Churches are not to be reformed wholesale. Changing people by the mass is no easy matter. Thousands are not converted in one day in our time. The true Christian advance is made by the slow, sure method of individual consecration to a life of holiness, and a faithful, consistent continuance in love to God and man, and humble obedience to law, human and divine.

Some complainers like to lay on the clergy the blame of the shortcomings of Christian churches.

A devout people will not long endure a clergy worldly or wicked. The clergy are, as it were, the blossom, the fruit of the plant, its ultimate result. As is the root, so will be the flower. As is the Church at large, so will the clergy be. Let the private Christians see to themselves that they are walking in the way of life, and there will grow up from among them, even at their own hearthstones, men who will preach with power, and live the holy life which becometh them who minister at the altar.

For individual self-examination and individual reformation there is no better guide for layman or priest than the searching words of the Master as He addressed the Seven Churches of Asia. The ascended Lord had spoken to disciples and apostles singly and severally, and now He comes with counsel and correction for the churches at large, for all time, collectively and separately.

"He that hath an ear, let him hear what the Spirit saith unto the churches." This solemn trumpet giveth no uncertain sound. It is "Onward, Christian soldier," through and through.

The message to the churches is for each individual member. The body is but an association of parts imbued with one life. So was it of old in Smyrna and Pergamos, in Sardis, in Philadelphia, in Thyatira, in Ephesus, in Laodicea.

That same message is addressed to us now. Somewhere in its warnings, as in its encouragements, there is a whisper to the soul of each one of us personally, and to the church of which we are a part. May God give us the grace to understand and to take home the needed lesson, to our instruction and growth in the religious life! Let us listen with the willing ear and the bowed head and the humble, penitent cry, "Lord, is it I?" even though at a Judas may be pointed the reproachful finger of the Redeemer.

And what has our Lord to say to us? Is there a Christian, filled with devout love and earnest zeal in the early days of his consecration, who has lost his first joy and devotedness amid the pleasures and cares and fond affections of this lower world? For him is the word, "Remember therefore from whence thou art fallen, and repent, and do the first works; or else I will come unto thee quickly, and will remove thy candlestick out of his place." What might sudden death be to the dull and darkened believer? If such wandering children really repent, even to them is promised that they shall "eat of the tree of life which is in the midst of the Paradise of God."

Is there a Christian whose works praise him who has passed through tribulation? Let him not boast himself as if his victory were already won. There may be more trouble in store for him. He must be *faithful unto death*, and then he will receive a "crown of life,"— a life that knows no "second death."

Is there a Christian living in the midst of them who love not God, who has yet kept the faith, and so fancies himself perfectly pure in doctrine and life? The Lord has "a few things" against him. He too must search his heart and repent, if he will not have the Lord "fight against him with the sword of his mouth." If he overcome, there are for him precious blessings, no promises that will gratify his pride or raise him publicly above his fellows, but a "new name," secretly given, that shall speak the approval of his Lord. "Let him that thinketh he standeth take heed lest he fall!"

Even the Christian to whom the Lord might say, "I know thy works and charity and service and faith and thy patience and thy works," may have a "few things" against him, hidden things known only to "the Son of God, who hath His eyes like unto a flame of fire." Faults, sins, temptations, that lurk deep down in the heart, must be burned out, given up in humble repentance. The good already done must not be relied on. There must be a continuance in well-doing, and the remembrance of the warning, "Hold fast till I come!"

Is there a Christian who has "a name to live and is dead," if he be not awakened by the voice of his Master? His "works are not perfect before God." The little good that is in him is ready to die. There may be one who has a name to live on earth as a Christian, and yet he is already blotted out of the Book of Life! Remember, thou who art fair without and foul within, "how thou hast received and heard, and hold fast and repent. If therefore thou shalt not watch, I will come on thee as a thief, and thou shalt not know what hour I will come upon thee."

Is there a Christian who "has a little strength"? He knows his weakness, however he may win the praise of men, and even the approval of his Lord. Be encouraged, faltering, trembling disciple. *Here* it is feebleness and stumbling, inward fears and outward falls. *Above*, thou shalt be "a pillar in the temple of thy God," something stable, fast, and sure. Thou shalt "go no more out." Thou shalt be marked with the name of thy God, as a sheep is marked with the name of his master. Thou wilt be at home in the New Jerusalem, safely folded at last!

Is there a so-called Christian who has no suspicion that all is not right with him, whose boast is, "I am rich, I lack nothing," while he is "poor and blind and naked"? Baptized into the Church of Christ, trained in sound doctrine and dogma, admitted to the sacred Supper of the Lord, he fancies his path the straightest road to heaven. He is yet a miserable outcast, a prodigal in his days of revelling. Happy if he awake to know that he is blind and hungry and naked, and to turn towards the home of the Merciful Father. The door is not yet closed. The door is never closed to the true penitent. From the depths of His love the Lord will say to this self-satisfied disciple, "I counsel thee to buy of me gold tried in the fire, that thou mayest be rich; and white raiment, that thou mayest be clothed, and that the shame of thy nakedness do not appear; and anoint thine eyes with eye-salve, that thou mayest see." It is the echo of the old appeal, "Why will ye die, ye house of Israel?" The Lord in His love may rebuke thee with sorrow and chasten thee with sore disappointment. He may awake thee with bitter pains, or show thee the face of sudden death, to rouse thee to a knowledge of thy condition. Once knowing thy poverty, thy shame, once repentant and humbled, the Lord will receive thee to be His forevermore.

To "overcome,"—that is the exhortation that rings out again and again from the "voice like many waters." It is only to "him that overcometh," not to him that goes bravely at first into the battle, that rich rewards are promised. Finally, the pledge is given, "To him that overcometh will I grant to sit with Me in my throne, even as I also overcame, and am set down with My Father in His throne."

Our merciful Elder Brother knows the difficulties and dangers of the way. He has tried our human life. He knows what it costs to overcome. He longs to say to us all, "Come, ye blessed of My Father, inherit the kingdom prepared for you before the foundation of the word!"

Lord, make us ready for Thy coming! Wash us from our sins! Sanctify us by Thy grace! Clothe us with the white garments of Thy righteousness! Receive us into Thine Everlasting Kingdom!

# Coming Again.

I. A Glad Welcome.
II. The Judge.

# Coming Again.

## I.

## A GLAD WELCOME.

*Behold, the Lord cometh with ten thousand of His saints.*
JUDE 14.

WHAT affectionate father, returning suddenly after a long absence, would like to have his children, instead of rejoicing at the sound of his footsteps, shrink away in terror, remembering their own wrong-doings, and fearing his pitiless wrath? Yet this is the spirit in which many believers honestly think of the coming of our Lord Jesus in the clouds of heaven. They fancy that humility is the ground of all their fears. Is it not rather their habitual unbelief in the willingness of God to forgive freely, and to grant abundantly the grace that shall transform the true follower into the likeness of his Master?

This timid, affrighted spirit was not inculcated by the Lord when on earth, nor afterwards by His disciples. The servants and friends of the

Bridegroom were to watch truly, and never relax in their faithful preparations for His coming, but they were to account that coming a cause of rejoicing. They were eagerly to meet Him, and comfort one another in tribulation with the promise of His glad appearing.

That great Advent, though described in words of majesty, is yet to be in the familiar beauty of the clouds of heaven, that can even now glow at the sunset hour with a transcendent richness of coloring and a mysterious, wonderful light that might well surround the triumphant return of our Lord and King.

He who gave us the blessing of family affection, the dear ties of friendship, and an enthusiasm for the great and good of bygone times, has not left out this human element in the joy of His coming. He is not to be alone, or only accompanied by those sinless, far-off beings, the holy angels. Even from the time of "Enoch the seventh from Adam," it was promised that the Lord should come to judge the world, with ten thousand of His saints about Him.

As in the pictures of some of the old painters the Madonna and the Infant Jesus may be seen looking out from a mist of sweet child-angels or cherubs, so we can imagine our Lord at His coming encompassed by the beautiful faces of our human brethren, "the just made perfect," their features luminous with the sacred brightness that may even now seem to transfigure the countenances of devout souls after long and true communion with God. Nor will those holy faces all be new and strange to us. Our dead who have passed from among us will be with the Lord at His coming. Beaming from eyes accustomed to see our Elder Brother and behold His glory will be their old love for us, increased, sanctified, perfected. Those eyes will be lit with glad recognition and the blessed knowledge that our trials and temptations are over, and we too are to taste the full blessedness in the presence of the Divine Master.

We sometimes shrink under the nervous fear of physical death, the wrenching asunder of body and soul, and the entering into a new state of existence. The valley of the shadow may perhaps be made dark to us by the thought of the friends we must leave to mourn and struggle, it may be, unprotected and unprovided for, when we are summoned to glory. We may have great plans for good, unrealized or uncompleted, that we feel it would be hard to leave begun and never finished. These misgivings must not be cherished. Our end may be the end and solemn closing of this earthly drama. We may have no death in store for us, no separation from loved ones, no career of usefulness cut short.

The time of the Lord's coming is the secret of the Father. We may have no future beyond the present hour. The sun, now high in the heavens, may have no common setting; it may pale before the brightness of the Sun of Righteousness.

Let us be found faithful in the little duties committed to our charge. Let us be among those who "love the Lord's appearing." Let us so live that from a joyful heart we may answer to the great announcement, "Lo, I come!" "Even so, come, Lord Jesus!"

## II.

## THE JUDGE.

*The Lord Jesus Christ, who shall judge the quick and the dead at His appearing.* — 2 TIMOTHY iv. 1.

AMONG the untold secrets of sensitive childhood, hidden in the little quivering heart, are those sudden wakings from sound sleep, in the dead of night, with a strong conviction that something terrible is happening. "Perhaps it is the Judgment Day!" whispers the accusing conscience. Real sins and small peccadilloes, in indiscriminate confusion, rise up before the memory of the affrighted child, filling it with a vague feeling of unutterable horror. The sublime picture of the solemn throne and the unspeakable glory of the Divine Presence flashes on the mind. The child, in dread waiting, hides its head till, strange to say, nature comes to its aid with the same sweet sleep as before that startled waking. The angels again watch over the little culprit, who opens his eyes in the morning refreshed, and with only a dim remembrance of that wild, troubled hour, as of a passing dream.

More terrible is the awakening which sometimes comes in maturer years, in a critical moment of utmost danger, or in the quiet sick-room, when the possible peril of the patient is written on the anxious faces round his bed. Here is often the same bewilderment as in the case of the child,—a sense of general sinfulness and certain doom, rather than penitence for particular sins and a sincere prayer for pardon. There may be a real call for mercy, and an honest purpose to lead a new life in case of recovery or escape from danger. More often it is a spurious conversion, like that of the wicked sailor who prays for help during his swift fall from the rigging, but resumes his cursing and his old life as soon as his feet firmly touch the deck.

A sudden deathbed repentance is always possible. The recovery of such apparent converts shows too often, however, that their temporary religiosity has been but a self-seeking, a longing for safety, with no horror of sin, and no true acceptance of our Lord as Saviour and Example and Purifier.

Doubtless, on the other side, there have been many sufferers who in the retirement of a protracted illness have passed from death unto life, and yet, through the weakness of mind and body consequent upon extreme prostration, have been unable to breathe even to the fond friends beside them a word of their new hope, or the separation they believe to be so near. The patient knows he could not bear a conversation that would deeply move him. He undertakes it no more than he does to get up and go about his room as usual. A wistful eye, a meaning glance, or a pressure of the hand may be all of which he is capable, save the sweet patience and lovingness that spring from a heart renewed. Our friends who have gone from us without a word of a new hope or a new Master may have been welcomed by rejoicing angels, and received to the kingdom of the Father by the merciful Son, who has seen their deep penitence and accepted their helpless reliance on Him at the eleventh hour.

What have old, experienced Christians to offer at the great tribunal after their years of stumbling along the narrow path? What but the "full, perfect, and sufficient sacrifice" of the Lamb once offered for the sins of the world?

For that great day when the secrets of all hearts shall be revealed, and the dead, small and great, shall stand before God, He has reserved a token of His infinite loving-kindness. One may have been long in the Christian life before one fully grasps the precious truth, known theoretically from childhood, that it is by Christ Jesus "that Man whom He has ordained," that God will judge the world. He who was "tempted in all points like as we are," He who has been child and youth and man, He who has had bitter enemies and faithless friends, He who washed the feet of His unstable disciples,— He, our Elder Brother, is to judge the poor children of earth, for whom He was willing to leave His Father's Home of glory and suffer a malefactor's death!

He who has heard our first faltering prayer to be led in the right way, He who has known our sins and our repentance, He who has accepted our poor offering of ourselves and all we are, and has been pleased to acknowledge us as His own, He who has companied with us all the days of our pilgrimage, He on whom we have leaned in sorrow and sickness and approaching death,— will not desert us when we stand before the great white throne, awaiting our final sentence. Because we are His, we shall share His home, and to His great name be the glory!

And what revelation have we of the test of discipleship in that awful hour? We hear of no questionings as to devout frames and glowing feelings, no mention but as warning, of having prophesied in His name.

What, then, is the test?

Christ has left on earth His types, His substitutes, His ambassadors,— the poor, the stranger, the widow, and the fatherless,— the helpless and distressed of the human race. What is written? "Inasmuch as ye have done it unto one of the least of these my brethren, ye have done it unto Me!"

Searching, solemn, condemning words! Lord, "deal not with us according to our sins, neither reward us according to our iniquities!" Give us all grace to love as brethren, and share with glad, grateful hearts the blessings Thou in mercy hast given us! Make us so to trust and follow Thee that we may dare to meet Thee, our Redeemer, as our Judge and King!

# In Glory.

   I. Rest.
  II. The Bride.
 III. The Holy City.

# In Glory.

## I.

### REST.

*And so shall we be ever with the Lord.* — 1 THESS. iv. 17.

TO be constantly in the society of the best beloved is for many human hearts the ideal of joy. It is for this the bride is willing to leave the sheltering arms of her mother, the well-tried faithful care of her father, and all the dear associations of her childhood's home.

And what is the result for the newly married pair? If their union has been founded on true affection, deep congeniality, and a common holy end and aim, both may find a happiness beyond what they ever dreamed of, — a happiness so pure and deep that it is wonderful that it is left in this poor world, for mere mortals to enjoy.

All this is true, but the expectation to be always with the beloved object is in this case a passing delusion. Time wears on, and the young husband, if he be a man to do his work in his day and generation, becomes involved in cares and interests and efforts that must take him during many hours of the day from the hearthstone. He returns, perhaps weary or perplexed or pre-occupied, his wife not his one thought, not even his time to be wholly offered to her, in his so-called leisure hours. Nor is she always ready for that endless *tête-à-tête* of her girlish imagination. A mother's cares and privileges have probably come upon her. Her little ones claim her attention and ever-increasing interest. They gather around her, each developing new needs, according to its age, and requiring a different training, adapted to its peculiar character and abilities.

The glad pair who started out to journey together hand-in-hand have found out that their life is no lingering pleasure promenade. It is a path thick-set with individual duties, where each must walk faithfully, gratefully welcoming the short time for mutual sympathy and converse that may be left amid the thronging occupations of every-day life.

There must come change and disappointment and sorrow to the Christian home, yet there we have the best idea and image of the eternal rest, where love will be the foundation of joy, and the presence of the Great Friend our highest bliss, and the glad fulfilment of His commands our ceaseless employment.

"There remaineth a rest for the people of God," but we are not to suppose it to be a state of self-indulgence and inactivity. "The Father worketh hitherto," and the angels are ministering spirits. Occupation will, no doubt, be provided for us, adapted to our new sphere and our new powers. With the universe at command, there will be no lack of space or opportunity for noble exertion.

Beauty and joy in abundance will, no doubt, be found in heaven. If here, in our poor schoolroom, we have the surpassing charms of nature in its manifold forms, above, where tasks have become willing service and discipline reward, what gladness there will be in obedience, what joy in exploring the wonders of God's endless creation!

Even the Home, where power and holiness and love are the essence of the Great Being who is the centre of its exalted bliss, would lose much of its blessedness if there we should be subject to change and uncertainty. How shadowed would be the brightest joy if the soul in the midst of its transports must echo its old cry in its sorrows, "How long, O Lord? How long?" The fixedness of our heavenly state, to be "ever with the Lord," is the great element of eternal rest. The very thought brings a sweet restfulness to our weary souls, here "tossed on life's tempestuous ocean." Let us take this great promise for our comfort amid the accepted disappointments and instabilities of our earthly home. Our longing shall at last be satisfied. We shall be ever with the Lord.

Let us see to it that we have characters, tastes, and affections modelled after our Elder Brother, who has gone before us and opened the way to the Heavenly Mansions.

A stranger cannot come *home* to the Father's house. It is only His child who can know that joy. Let us not be distant, suspicious strangers towards our loving Lord, but here obedient, trustful children; and then none of us will come short of entering into the rest that remaineth for the people of God.

## II.

## THE BRIDE.

*The marriage of the Lamb has come, and His wife has made herself ready.* — REV. xix. 7.

NO royal bridegroom who makes his wife a queen bestows on her as great an honor as that which she shares with the humblest maid who takes the marriage vows. Our Lord has set the human bride as a type of the invisible Church, the redeemed souls who are to be His in His eternal home.

He has chosen them, and they have given their free consent to be His, and His alone.

What a whisper this is for the earthly bride on her marriage morning! She is to be an image of the sanctified Church of God, to be one day presented to the Lord "without spot or wrinkle or any such thing." What a motive for one who is leaving her girlhood behind her, to leave with it her old faults, her old sins, and to begin her new life in charity and faith, in childlike reliance on God alone, determined to be in the coming relation holier and therefore happier than ever before.

The humblest bride comes not to the altar in the every-day dress of this working world. Adorned as befits the occasion, she is given to her husband not even in the garments that have served for this feast or that merry-making. There must be the freshness as of a new creation about her. She is leaving her past behind her. All things for her are to be new. In how many lands she wears the modest veil that sets her apart! She is already not her own, not belonging in the same sense as before to her family and friends and the outer world. She is to be given to him whose name she is to bear, and whose home is to be henceforward hers.

And the Bride, the Church of Christ? Because she is loved, because she has been bought at the price of the Bridegroom's humiliations and sufferings, and is confident of her welcome to His Home, is she in a kind of slipshod indifference to await in her earth-stained garments the coming of the Lord? Is she to look forward to the sound of the solemn trump with a kind of self-sufficient composure, as if it were an every-day affair? Not so do we learn from the Scriptures. It is written, "The marriage of the Lamb has come, and His wife has made herself ready."

There is a presumption that speaks of the

abounding love of Christ and His free forgiveness, as if we might continue in sin because grace has so abounded. Knowing that we have nought to fear, we must still have a horror of sin, a tender sensitiveness that there may be no taint on our bridal garment, itself the gift of the Lord.

# III.

## THE HOLY CITY.

*The Holy City, New Jerusalem.* — REV. xxi. 22.

THE Bible is full of surprises for us. It does not seem strange that the story of man, like the history of civilization, should begin in the open air, with human beings surrounded by fruitful trees, and in free companionship with nature in all its forms. That the story of man should end, like the history of civilization, in the magnificent city, is indeed a surprise.

Cities, as we know them, do not seem to give us an image of the Home of the Blessed. Yet in the promise of the Holy City, New Jerusalem, we have forced upon us one of the great lessons of Christianity. The true religion is not a religion of selfishness and solitude, but of love and sympathy and companionship. How can we describe outward beauty to the blind? How can we make the deaf understand the loving, touching cadences of the human voice, or the delight that gladdens the ear awake to music? What can we, mortals of clay, know of the glories of heaven, or the joys of that holy place? Little indeed! It is only by its being likened to things with which we are familiar that we can catch a glimpse of its glory and purity.

In the city we have the highest forms of development to which man can attain in works of beauty and splendor from the skilful hand or the thinking mind; yet it has its horrible taint of sin, — sin in its most rank and vigorous growth.

In the Holy City there will be nothing that defileth, no dark and gloomy shadow. In the midst of its dazzling magnificence there will appear in its bright streets no long funeral train, with its solemn hearse and mocking pageantry. No mourners, no tears, no secret anguish will be there. There will be no care-wrinkled, sin-marked faces in the glad throngs of the golden streets. No one there will pine for dear ones across the wide ocean, for in the Holy City there will be "no more sea" to divide true hearts. There will be no crime there, no night when deeds are done that would shun detection and shame.

The great evil of the earthly city that flourishes even in the daylight, will not enter the pearly gates. He that "loveth and maketh a lie" dare not venture within the jewelled walls of the New Jerusalem.

The lie acted and spoken, that drags down the

soul of the man of business, will not be there. The social lie, that speaks fair words, when the heart is full of bitterness, or that flatters and cringes to win the favor of those who have long purses or sit in high places, will not be there. The beggar's lie will not be there, to harden the heart of speaker and hearer. The religious lie will not be there. No one will solemnly promise in that Holy of Holies to keep the law of God and walk in purity and truth, and then turn thoughtlessly again to his old ways of folly or sin. No one will sit down to the supper of the Lamb, and rise up to profane His holy name. There will not be the acted lie of the worshippers who seem to pray and praise, while their thoughts are on pleasure or business or anxious care. No one there will be outwardly proper and seemly and righteous, with a foul and evil heart within.

Away with the lie *here*, if we would live hereafter in the glad presence of the God of Truth!

It is not alone in negatives that the Holy City is described. We have its walls flashing with jewels, its gates of pearls, its golden streets, its river that makes a garden in its midst, where trees with healing leaves bear perpetually their fruit in the glad light that knows no shadow.

All that we can imagine of outward beauty will be there. "Eye hath not seen nor ear heard, neither hath it entered into the heart of man to conceive the things which God hath prepared for them that love Him."

This world with its worldliness will have passed away. The covetousness that is idolatry will find no place in the Holy City. The garments given by the Lord our Righteousness will be signs of purity, not of pride. "They that overcome shall walk with Him in white."

The Lord God and the Lamb will be that City's light. There will be nothing to hide there. Accepted in the Elder Brother, the saints shall see the face of God, and not shrink from the All-seeing Eye, but rejoice in the light of His countenance.

All happiness that is innocent will be there, all that is ennobling, exalting, all that is holy and pure.

"The nations shall bring their glory and honor into it. Not that the torn standards captured in war, and the records of bloody victories, will be offered to God. The *men* who have really been an honor to their native land and its true glory, will be there. What converse there will be with the great and good of all time! God's best works, noble souls!"

What worship there will be there! Here, where we are but creatures of a day, some of us have heard in the great gatherings of Christians from the wide world, in the grandest of its cities, prayer and praise go up at once from thousands of adoring worshippers, from every clime, and can dimly, very dimly, imagine something of the chorus of holy halleluias in heaven!

There will be music there. God, who gave the human voice its sweet modulations, and formed the subtle laws of sounds that can be grouped to harmony and melody, will have music around His throne, music among the rejoicing saints and angels.

There will be love in the Holy City. Earth's best joy will be there, exalted, purified, made holy and eternal.

There we shall be with the Elder Brother, in His glory, as He was with us in His humiliation. There He who hath loved us, will love us unto the end. There we poor orphans of earth will find our Father, and be welcomed to His Home. There we shall be in the presence of our Almighty King, the All-powerful, the All-wise, whose name is Love.

What a city that will be, "whose Builder and Maker is God"!

"Here we have no continuing city." Cities rise, cities fall, and their inhabitants are as the dust of the earth. The Holy City, New Jerusalem, is the *Eternal* Home of the redeemed in Christ Jesus.

# INDEX ACCORDING TO TEXTS.

## Before the World Was.

| | |
|---|---|
| SELF-SACRIFICE. | "The glory which I had with the Father before the world was." |
| CREATION. | "All things were made by Him." |
| STEADFASTNESS. | "The Lamb slain from the foundation of the world." |
| HUMILITY AND OBEDIENCE. | "My Father." |

## A Child.

| | |
|---|---|
| THE BABE. | "The Babe lying in a manger." |
| THE CHILD JESUS. | "Thy Holy Child Jesus." |
| FORMS. | "Thus it becometh us to fulfil all righteousness." |
| A NAME. | "Thou shalt call His name Jesus." |
| A WIDE CIRCLE. | "We have seen His star in the East, and are come to worship Him." |
| BOYS. | "And He went down with them and came to Nazareth, and was subject unto them." |

## Ministering.

| | |
|---|---|
| TEMPTATION. | "Himself having suffered, being tempted." |
| BABES IN CHRIST. | "And He called unto Him whom He would, and they came unto Him." |

| | |
|---|---|
| Recreation. | "And both Jesus was called and His disciples to the wedding." |
| Seekers. | "Nicodemus, which at the first came to Jesus by night." |
| Tired. | "Jesus being wearied with His journey." |
| Relatives. | "And when Jesus was come into Peter's house, He saw his wife's mother laid, and sick of a fever." |
| Faults. | "Why are ye so fearful?" |
| Mourners. | "He had compassion on her." |
| Self-Denial. | "I will not send them away fasting, lest they faint by the way." |
| Economy. | "Gather up the fragments that remain, that nothing may be lost." |
| Opposition. | "Neither did His brethren believe on Him." |
| Deformity. | "Master, who did sin, this man or his parents, that he was born blind?" |
| Parents. | "Lord, have mercy on my son!" |
| Seeming Death. | "He is dead!" |
| The Nursery. | "Whoso receiveth one such little child in my name, receiveth me." |
| The Capital. | "He beheld the city, and wept over it." |
| Workmen. | "I have finished the work Thou gavest me to do." |
| Constancy. | "Having loved His own which were in the world, He loved them unto the end." |
| Forgiveness. | "Father, forgive them; they know not what they do." |
| Trust. | "Into Thy hands, I commend my spirit." |

### Crucified.

"And sitting down, they watched Him there."

### Risen.

| | |
|---|---|
| The Grave. | "They have taken away my Lord, and I know not where they have laid Him." |
| In Remembrance. | "In remembrance of Me." |
| Vision. | "Then were the disciples glad when they saw the Lord." |

| | |
|---|---|
| By the Way. | "What manner of communications are these that ye have one to another?" |
| The Old Testament. | "Then opened He their understanding, that they might understand the Scriptures." |
| The Sheep. | "Feed my lambs! Feed my sheep!" |
| Daily Bread. | "Children, have ye any meat?" |

## Ascended.

| | |
|---|---|
| Lost and Found. | "He lifted up His hands, and blessed them. . . . While He blessed them, He was parted from them, and carried up into heaven?" |
| A Miracle. | "When the Comforter is come, whom I will send unto you from the Father." |
| Union. | "That they may be one." |
| Dying Eyes. | "Behold, I see the heavens opened, and the Son of Man standing at the right hand of God!" |
| A Voice from Heaven. | "Much more shall not we escape if we turn away from Him that speaketh from heaven." |
| Persecution. | "I am Jesus, whom thou persecutest." |
| Penitents. | "I have much people in this city." |
| Gentiles. | "Depart! for I will send thee far hence unto the Gentiles." |
| Cheer. | "Be of good cheer, Paul!" |
| Weakness. | "My strength is made perfect in weakness." |
| Priests. | "We have a great High-Priest." |
| Churches. | "I, Jesus, have sent mine angel to testify unto you these things in the churches." |

## Coming Again.

| | |
|---|---|
| A Glad Welcome. | "Behold, the Lord cometh with ten thousand of His sain's!" |
| The Judge. | "The Lord Jesus Christ, who shall judge the quick and the dead at His appearing." |

## In Glory.

Rest. "And so shall we be ever with the Lord."
The Bride. "The marriage of the Lamb has come, and His wife has made herself ready."
The Holy City. "The Holy City, New Jerusalem."

www.ingramcontent.com/pod-product-compliance
Lightning Source LLC
Chambersburg PA
CBHW030820230426
43667CB00008B/1303